Where Laugh Touches Tears

WHERE LAUGH TOUCHES TEARS

Selected Works From the COMPAS Writers & Artists in the Schools Program

Edited by
Sigrid Bergie

Illustrations by
Barbara Kreft

COMPAS
Writers & Artists in the Schools
1991

Publication of this book is generously supported by the Sven and C. Emil Berglund Foundation, dedicated in memory of C. Emil Berglund.

COMPAS programs are made possible in part by grants provided by the Minnesota State Arts Board, through an appropriation by the Minnesota State Legislature. In the past year, the COMPAS Writers & Artists in the Schools program has received generous support from the Hugh J. Andersen Foundation, the Ashland Oil Foundation, the Cargill Foundation, the International Multifoods Charitable Foundation, Land O'Lakes and US WEST Communications.

As always, we are grateful for the hundreds of excellent teachers throughout Minnesota who sponsor COMPAS Writers & Artists in the Schools residencies. Without their support and hard work, the writers and artists would not weave their magic, and the student work we celebrate in this book would not spring to life.

Additional thanks are due to Jo Svendsen, WAITS Program Associate, for her tireless efforts at keeping the program wheels rolling and to Carol Bergelund, COMPAS Secretary, for her keyboard wizardry.

ISBN 0-927663-17-1

Illustrations copyright © 1991 Barbara Kreft
Text copyright © 1991 COMPAS
All rights reserved. No portion of this book may be reprinted or reproduced without the prior written permission of COMPAS, except for brief passages cited in reviews.

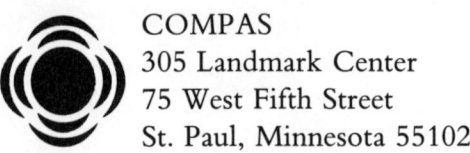

COMPAS
305 Landmark Center
75 West Fifth Street
St. Paul, Minnesota 55102

Molly LaBerge, Executive Director
Daniel Gabriel, Director, Writers & Artists in the Schools

Table of Contents

Sigrid Bergie — *Introduction* — ix

I. Broken Down from All the Rainbows

Molly Gilberg	*Broken Down From All the Rainbows*	2
Jason Helm	*Growing Up*	3
Derek Schluessler	*On the Day I Was Born*	5
Kara Marie Dinkel	*In My Childhood Drawing*	6
Dina Fuerstenberg	*Lost Eras*	7
Jessica Carlson	*Bike Lesson*	8
Malla Lofgren	*Newborn Baby*	9
Zack Chapman	*Baby*	10
Christina Joeckel	*I Am Like a Flower Blooming*	12
Joshua Pierce	*Always*	13
Kara Adams	*When I Was a Little Kid*	14
Tonya Peterson	*A Place to Play*	19

II. The Truth of a Stone

Jim Vanderbeek	*Days of a Stone*	22
Eva Curry	*. . . And the Poem Said . . .*	23
Barry Jesinoski	*The Truth of a Stone*	24
Tammy Anderson	*The One Who Judges Jewels*	25
Missy Lund	*Life*	27
Kari Spielman	*The Wind Spirits*	28
Travis Howard	*The True Meaning of Life*	29
Liz Hook	*The Perfect World*	33
Nkoyo E. Iyamba	*Jumping Off Cliffs at the Boundary Waters*	36
Rich Kirk	*Stone vs. Heart*	37
Ryan Bigelow	*Self Portrait*	38

John Mitsch &		
Ricky Sullivan	*The Mystical Eye*	39
Scott Hella	*The Sea Shell*	40
Mara Segal	*Tip-Toes of a Crescent Moon*	41
Hannah Blair	*Moon*	42

III. MY BROTHER WILL NEVER BE A FARMER

Aaron Weckman	*My Little Brother*	44
John Kent	*My Sewing Sister*	45
Brian Daniels	*River of Chocolate*	46
Sean Bauch	*My Family is Like a Sports Car*	47
Virginia Laursen	*All About Me*	48
Brigit Riley	*Don't Pull a Brigit*	49
Adam Cerling	*Picture Puzzled*	50
Azra Babar	*The Sting*	51
Marni Kramer	*A Train Going East*	53
Jared Detloff	*My Uncle Barry*	57
Fong Inthavixay	*Inside My Family*	58
Teri Firkins	*David*	59
Nkenge Shakir	*Brat*	61
Michael Spencer	*Days of Our Lives*	62
Jessica McKinley	*A Lesson From Grandmom*	63
Liz Goodman	*The Race*	64
Christy Boraas	*The Old One*	67
Aaron Peter	*Grandpa*	68
Kelsey Olson	*Sewing As Fast As a Car*	69
Orin Johnson	*Serenity*	70

IV. A MINGLING

Cindy Skogerboe	*What Is It?*	74
Lori DeLaitsch	*Be A Good Poem*	76
Dee Dee Budde	*A Mingling*	77
Tracey Muralt	*The Mississippi*	78
Missy Mollick	*Old Mississippi River Songs*	79
Matthew P. Borg	*POP, POP, Crunch, Crunch*	80
Rachel Breitenbach	*Kitchen Songs*	81
Jennifer Wetherbee	*Low B-flat*	82
Rachel Squires	*Flowers Around Me*	84
Magenta Miller	*The Telephone*	85

John Poegel	*A Little Anger Sometimes*	86
Natalie White	*Call It Selective Hearing*	87
Makalah Haessler	*Chapter Two: The Fortune Cookie*	88
Andrew Burth	*The Brazil Nut With Nine Faces*	89
Dan Compton	*The Hand*	90
Dan Schwarz	*Hands*	91
Michelle Gilbert	*Blessed*	92
Sotearit Chak	*Little Dipper*	93
Stacy Reed	*Cassiopeia*	94
Minne Vang	*Big Dipper*	95
Nina Raulerson	*Orion*	96
Nancy Kadlec	*Along With My Mind*	97
Shayne B. Meyer	*My Club House*	98
Clayton Engen	*Dear Lake*	99

V. IT FLIES WITH FEATHERS

Eric Andrews	*Gold Sparrow*	102
Carolyn Hudalla	*The Sign of the Dove*	103
Tony Housey	*Birds of Prey*	104
Mychal Lynn Anderson	*Panther*	105
Naomi Smith	*Reflections on a Summer Afternoon*	107
Tamara Eagle	*If I Were an Eagle*	109
Aaron Morrison	*A Streak of Beauty*	110
Jeremy Stewart	*The Butterfly*	112
Mark Gudmastad	*The Deer Who Followed Me*	113
Jennie Grundeen	*My Friend*	114
Gina Jaszczak	*Love*	115

VI. FOREVER DREAMS

Nicole Kolashinski	*My Imagination*	118
Karen Gilbertson	*Forever Dreams*	119
Deanne Kociemba	*My Hands Jump*	120
Kevin Sieben	*Hand*	121
Chaitra Wirta	*The Tic-Tac-Toe Aliens*	122
Judi Fay	*The Search*	124
Aaron Weiche	*Because*	126
Shawna Beise	*The Dream*	127
Craig Sweet	*The Goddess of Darkness*	128
Jennifer Fenton	*Childhood*	129

Nikki Stevens	*The Door is Round and Open*	130
Dustin Blonigen	*Magic Present*	131

VII. WHERE LAUGH TOUCHES TEARS

Gretchen Mollers	*To Keep Happiness*	134
Erika Olson	*Saver of Life*	135
Katrina Cranston	*For You, My Friend*	136
Kelly McGuire	*It All Laughs*	137
Chad Carlson	*Today's World*	138
Monique Farness	*Teddy Bear*	139
Matt Jensvold	*Being A Child*	140
Colleen Pemberton	*Asleep Forever*	141
Georgina Sisk	*A Lovely Dream*	142
Cory Busse	*Masks*	143
Diane Strandlund	*Maybe This Way is Better*	144
Heather Milless	*More Than Just a Regular Day*	147
Ranae Wayrynen	*Ranae*	149
Jake Mulligan	*After Surgery*	150
Jessica Koll	*Losing A Pet*	151
Jamie Ager	*Matching Pair of Eyes*	152
Tricia Roberts	*Red Licorice*	153
Kelli Beitlich	*Where Laughter Touches Tears*	155

Author Index	157
School Index	161
Program Writers 1990–1991	164

Introduction

Where Laugh Touches Tears is a gift to the reader from the students, teachers and writers who participated in COMPAS Writers & Artists in the Schools residencies during the 1990–1991 school year. There are hundreds of students' poems and prose pieces which should, but do not, appear here — yet their energy vibrates in the book's spirit.

This book is a reciprocal gift between writer and reader. Somehow, miraculously, a story or poem that comes from the writer's soul calls from the reader that which is deepest in his or her soul, and together from our innermost selves, we create a story or poem that neither of us could have alone.

It is a reciprocal gift for us adults to live and teach in the presence of children — their worlds are more intense and profound than most adults. Someone once said (perhaps it was a Chinese philosopher) that the final stage in life — which few achieve — is to become a mature child. When they are encouraged to be true and free, children easily open up to write with wisdom and poignancy along with sheer enjoyment of words, sounds and imaginings. To enter the worlds of such densely complicated creatures is magic.

While editing this book, I was moved to laugh and cry for the simplicity, harmony and depth of feeling in so many poems and stories. So it was difficult to make the final selections for the anthology — and even more difficult to write this introduction because you ought to be feasting on the book right now, all right, already!

My wish is that the writers represented here and all young writers will continue to write, to create and, at least, to create their lives with the honesty and beauty of *Where Laugh Touches Tears*.

Sigrid Bergie
August, 1991

Broken Down from All the Rainbows

Broken Down from All the Rainbows

Childhood is like a crayon
always being used
and being
broken down from
all the rainbows.

But when someone
picks you up and
sharpens you until
there's nothing left,
you are an adult.

Molly Gilberg :: Grade 4
Barnum Elementary School :: Barnum

Growing Up

I remember the old white house
with the huge back yard.
That's where I used to go to fight dragons
and search for unicorns
and fly.
The trees were a thick jungle
full of mystery.

One day I saw a beautiful butterfly in
my jungle.
It was as blue as the deep sea,
with blood red stripes.
Its wings were pursed together like a mother's warm lips
giving a gentle kiss.
It did not move.
It was magical.
I reached over to carefully pick it off
the tree.
Still, it remained motionless.
I had it in my hand.
The magic was mine!
The warm feel of life pulsed through
my fingers and into the paralyzed butterfly . . .
And then I dropped it.
Its soul was restored.
Wings opened like a Chinese fan.
It glided through the air with such grace.
I was ready to follow it,
but I could not fly.
I tried, but I could not fly.

I went to my special place less and less.
It wasn't the same.
The magic flew away with the butterfly,
and I could not follow it.

Jason Helm :: Grade 9
John Adams School :: Rochester

On the Day I Was Born

    On the day I was born,
the huskies in the arctic hauled with all their might.
    On the day I was born,
the eagles flew high, high in the air and screamed
at the top of their lungs.
    On the day I was born,
all of the whales swam wildly spraying water everywhere.
    On the day I was born,
civilization sprang heavily into the world.
    On the day I was born.
I was dropped from the top of the world
and hung on with life.

Derek Schluessler :: Grade 4
Christa McAuliffe Elementary School :: Hastings

In My Childhood Drawing

In my childhood drawing
I see a ball that rolls
slowly along the ground like
a glob of Jello, as if frightened
at the foot that is about to
kick it.

I see trees that look like
extending arms looking up
at the sky waiting for rain.
My brother (the oldest), my
sister (the second oldest), my
two cousins Steven and
Michael—and myself—are
playing kickball in our front
yard.

When I look back on this
drawing of mine, I see radiant
colors blooming everywhere.
I see the lush green grass trying
to stand straight up from where
it was once stepped on.
The trees are bending and swaying
just a little in the warm and sunny day.

And as I sit here looking back on this drawing
I can still smell the sweet and delicious aroma
of fresh baked chocolate chip cookies. And I hear
the faint voice of my mother saying,
"Cookies, anyone?"

Kara Marie Dinkel :: Grade 6
Long Prairie Elementary School :: Long Prairie

Lost Eras

Back in the days when
my closet was another world,
and my Beth doll was my only baby
until Dad broke her head off.
Those were the days when
The Stray Cats and Elvis were all I played
on the record player in my yellow room.
Back in the nights when
fears of monsters under the bed,
fears of mosquitos we smooshed
on the doghouse ceiling
coming back to life,
and still believing that my hamster *did*
move in my hands that night,
and fears of him buried alive.
Those were the nights when
Missy, Tracy, Kristy and I
prepared for our weddings to
my brother "Ace," Chris, Mike and "Doodlebug"
and the other girls had white curtain dresses,
but my flimsy red dress was worn by my mom
who gave me a little brother
instead of the sister she knew I wanted.
Back before the summer changed to winter,
and the swingset covered with snow,
and we had to play in Dorothy's garage.
Back before "Ace" outgrew his name,
and "Doodlebug" quit coming around.
Before Tracy and Missy moved away,
before Beth died and I was forced
   to grow up.

Dina Fuerstenberg :: Grade 11
Stillwater High School :: Stillwater

BIKE LESSON

When I see my old bike, I become
five years old. I am wobbly,
weaving back and forth.
My father's grip
is my only balance. I pray
he won't let go.
My legs are spinning,
my father's panting, my stomach
tells me that he will soon
let go. I turn
to look and as I crash, I know
I am on my own.

Jessica Carlson :: Grade 4
Royal Oaks Elementary School :: Woodbury

Newborn Baby

I open my eyes, big eyes and black, and look
right in front of me. I scream and
yell but they just "ooh" and "aah." Saying
how cute I am. People cutting cords
and fiddling with me. New clothes,
a big shopping center of their choice.
Everyone going close to my face
making noises. A nightmare of memories,
a circle of people reaching for me.
Sticking food and things in my face,
I am a zoo animal getting fed peanuts.

Malla Lofgren :: Grade 5
Shirley Hills Elementary School :: Mound

Baby

The baby comes glowing into the
overwhelming world. It is new
and fragile like a crumbling autumn
leaf. The fingers so small and weak
like a meaningless twig in the mists
of death. The face is so sweet and
innocent like a bright new moon.

This little bundle appears from
the sweet and harmlessness of nature
like the increase of a fresh snowfall.

It leaves a wondrous joy in
even those who have an impenetrable
heart of stone. It seems to
leave an unexplainable joy in its
path. It can lift even the
dreadest of gloominess. It is
the spark that brings things
to life and it's the spirit that
moves the earth.

The baby is as young as
the light pricks you feel in
the rain.

The baby's hunger is only for
love and affection.

The baby's arm is like a
rubbery snake. Its toes
are like little agates shining
on a wet beach.

Zack Chapman :: Grade 5
Tanglen Elementary School :: Minnetonka

I Am Like a Flower Blooming

My head is a home for my brain.
My blood flows like a river rushing.
In my fingers there are apples
falling and tingling. When I run, it's
like a train zooming by. My eyes are
like chocolate candy. My voice is as loud as
a lawn mower. When I was born I was
a roaring lion. When I die I will be flowers
closing up. My hair grows like snakes
falling down my back. My thoughts are clouds
blowing in the wind. All I want
is for summer to come.

Christina Joeckel :: Grade 3
Pullman Elementary School :: St. Paul Park

Always

I am like a little humming bird
In the sky always exploring
Everywhere
I am like a computer
Always thinking about something
I am like a wolf
Dancing in the moonlight every
night
I am like a star
Always moving from place to place
I am like the pages in a book
Always flipping through things
I am not a train.

Joshua Pierce :: Grade 4
Woodbury Elementary School :: Woodbury

When I Was a Little Kid

Now that I am a teenager, I look back at my childhood and wonder how it went so fast. On the other hand if you ask my mother, she will tell you that it seems like I have been here forever.

From what they tell me, I was born at Fairview Hospital in Minneapolis. My mother claims that I was four weeks late, but they never checked with my secretary to see if the scheduled time was mutually convenient. I had bright fuzzy orange hair. Orange and pink clash, so my mother never color-coded me. No one knew I was a girl. I'm sure this left deep psychological scars.

The first thing I remember is living on a farm in Wisconsin. The chickens were bigger than I was and they would chase me. The mail box was a long way down the road. The calves ran loose in the yard, and one time one came into the house through the open patio door. From a tall wooden highchair, I presided over the dinner table. My table manners weren't quite polished. It is a good thing that they had a dog to pick up the food that missed my mouth.

When I was one and one half, we moved to a mustard-colored fourplex. The plumbing had been added after the house was built. The bathroom was in a lean-to porch, and it froze up in the winter. We went to the gym at the college to shower. The only heat in the place was from a gas heater in the kitchen. When it was cold, we slept in the kitchen.

During that summer when I turned two, I became the proud owner of a secondhand tricycle. The kid upstairs had a cheap new one. Mine was built like a tank, and while his fell apart over the summer, mine lasted for all the years until my knees hit the handle bars and I passed it on to my second cousin. We held tricycle races up and down the sidewalk. Sometimes we would trade and I would ride his blue tricycle and he would ride my red one.

On hot sunny days my mother would equip me with a plastic pail of water and an old paint brush and tell me to paint the sidewalk. By the time I reached one end, the other end would be dry, so I would run back and start over.

Our main transportation was a bicycle with a seat on the back for me. The seat was yellow and it had a seat belt and a place for my feet. I remember riding behind my mother, and as we went we would chant the alphabet, numbers, the months, the days of the week, rhymes, poems and songs. On the days it rained she wrapped me in a lawn and leaf bag and clothespinned it at my neck. That covered not only me but the seat and whatever I was carrying. Sometimes I carried a stuffed animal, sometimes my backpack for day care, sometimes I carried a small bag of groceries from the store.

In the late summer the temptation of our neighbors' tomato garden became too much for me. I could be found in the early morning sitting among the plants eating cherry tomatoes. The neighbors thought I was adorable and told me to help myself so no amount of scolding on my mother's part had any effect. There was a door to the outside in my room and in the early morning I could escape silently. When I returned home with dirt on the feet of my bunny pajamas and tomato dribbled down the front, she knew immediately that I had been out and about.

On the refrigerator I had magnetic letters. The first letter I learned was J. The J was green. It stood for Jeremy, my friend's name. Green Jeremy J, I would chant. Next I learned K, the letter for Kara. Pretty soon I knew all of them.

I had a goldfish named Goober. Goober was black. I carried Goober around in a clear plastic cup with plastic wrap on the top, because I did not want to leave Goober at home. Goober came to daycare and the grocery store and everywhere else I went. Goober was a very hardy fish.

When I was three we moved back to Minneapolis. In an effort to expose me to culture, I was enrolled in ballet class. My stage debut was in a red and white tutu, dancing with six other disoriented three year olds, to "Babes in Toyland." My dancing career was cut short by my inability to distinguish left from right. The teacher was determined that we would all turn the same way and I found her inflexibility too confining for my creative nature.

At three it was also decided that I would take Swimming Lessons. This was when it became clear that I was not living in a democracy, but a dictatorship. My mother tells an amusing story about my first "water babies" class at the "Y" when I was about nine months old. While the other mothers and babies were happily bobbing up and down, I screamed in terror and left claw marks on her neck trying to keep out of the water. At three my opinion of swimming had not changed much. I began the class with suspicious skepticism. The lessons were outdoors in the early morning. Rows of little purple children sat shivering on the edge as the instructor came and put us in the water one by one. My mother firmly believes this sort of torture builds character.

When I was four my mother took me on the first in a series of camping trips. My camping memories run one year into another. One time we were in South Dakota in the Black Hills. We went to a park with dinosaur statues. I did not realize how hot they were from sitting in the sun, and one of my most vivid childhood memories is burning my bottom on a hot dinosaur. Almost every year we stopped at Mt. Rushmore, walked up the hill, bought a postcard, took a picture, watched the movie about how it was done, drank from the water fountain, walked down the hill, and sat in traffic on the way out.

On another trip we stayed at Jellystone Park in the Wisconsin Dells. Every other family with small children in North America was there that same week. There was a line for everything. They showed Yogi Bear movies outdoors after dark. At that campground I swam across the deep end of the pool for the first time. Also in the Wisconsin Dells I went down my first water slide. I liked it so much we stayed all day.

In Glacier National Park there was snow in the mountains all summer. We made a snowman, in our shorts. We drove to the top of the Continental Divide in the fog and watched the sun come up. I remember posing for a picture on the edge of the Grand Canyon. I was sure I was going to fall. We swam in a lake that was formed by a melting glacier. Cold does not begin to describe it. Every body part in the water had no feeling. I have a rock I brought home from that lake.

In Yellowstone I remember Old Faithful. Every year we arrived right after it went off and had to wait another 59 minutes because you can't drive all the way to Yellowstone and not have a picture of Old Faithful. I remember the clear blue water boiling out of the ground. We saw moose and bear. Every time an animal stepped out of the woods, traffic would come to a halt as everyone got their camera and gave chase until the animal stepped back into the woods.

We could not camp in Yellowstone because you have to have a hard top camper because of the bears and we had a small blue tent. I became very good at helping to set the tent up every night and take it down in the morning. At night it was my job to kill the last mosquito in the tent. Every time it rained I was overcome by temptation and I touched the top of the tent, and, in the spot I touched rain would leak in. This was contrary to my mother's good advice. I'm sure it was an early sign of my scientific mind.

Camping was a low budget affair and another vivid memory is eating beans from a can and mixing powdered milk in a cup and then pouring the Cheerios in. We sang until we lost our voices. We watched the stars until the mosquitos drove us into the tent. We watched sunrises and sunsets in the mountains that were magnificent.

Another thing that happened when I was between three and seven was that I had a babysitter named Rita. There were four kids that were at Rita's house. I was the oldest by one year. Christy and Jered were a year younger and Alyssa was a baby when I started. We were all together for five years until Rita got another job when Christy went to first grade. I still miss her.

At Rita's house we baked bread and each took a little loaf home. We planted flower bulbs in the fall and tulips came up in the spring. We rode everywhere in her green Slugbug. She took us to the beach and I got sunburnt. In the back yard we made mud with the hose. We found worms in the mud and sorted them and put them in the garden. I swung on her swing until I threw up; and learned first hand why it is a good idea to take turns.

Rita's husband Jay was home during the day. All the little kids would trail after him and "help" him as he worked on the car or built things. Once he built a deck in the back yard. I remember sitting underneath it with Christy and watching her eat mud. Of course I never ate mud. Every kid would take a tool and we would all head different directions. Jay's sense of humor probably saved us from mass infanticide.

Every year at Christmas time my mother made me a dress. I helped pick out the fabric and I watched her make them. She would use the same fabric to make an outfit for my current favorite doll or stuffed animal. My all time favorite dress was grey with cream colored lace and pearl buttons and ruffles. One was dark green with a white pinafore. One was brown with cream eyelet.

Every year in the summer I had my picture taken at a studio. I usually wore my Christmas dress. One year I had my rabbit in the picture with me. Twice our dog Crumpet was in the picture. When I was three I clutched my soccer ball.

When I was five my mother built a loft bed for my room. She built shelves and a desk. When I was eight we built a fort in the back yard. I helped design it. It has a ladder, working windows, a trap door, carpet, curtains and furniture — all made by my mother. She built a condo for my rabbits with shelves at different levels for them to perch on. It has nest boxes and a removable base. She built a boathouse at our cabin and I helped pound nails in the roof. She built a new outhouse (at the lake) because the old one was falling down. She built a deck, a wall, some shelves, a fence, and she poured a cement floor. I helped stir the cement with a hoe.

Kara Adams :: Grade 7
Blake Middle School :: Hopkins

A Place to Play

Whispering wind blows through the hollow trees.
It looks just like a normal forest
but not these trees, they're mine.
Way back in our pasture they stand
All the leaves have fallen
When I was young, I played there
Sometimes with others, sometimes alone.
A big group of trees was all it was
but to me inside I saw much more.
To go back would be a dream
But this cannot happen.
For I go back there many times,
But never see the things I saw.
Back then I dreamed of growing up
I could make up my whole future
just the way I wanted it
I could be whoever and do whatever I
wanted. It was my world.
I was always accepted there.
But now as I grow up
I dream of being young,
back in my little wooden house.
Being what I wanted to be
not what the world has made me.

Tonya Peterson :: Grade 12
Long Prairie High School :: Long Prairie

The Truth of a Stone

Days of a Stone

Go inside a stone
That would be my way
crack the walls of the crystal
let light strike at sunrise
work your way in a dream
and picture yourself at a door
let your twilight grief seep through
your blood
enter in with a scorch of hope
the sky is blue, and with a scream of hell.
The seed is wet, the wall is clear
the pearl looks like an eye
who is watching from midnight to dawn
melt into the ashes
walk with the colors
nest yourself in a hot bed.
Listen to the sleet as it drips
from a hand of blood
look inside to see if it is clear
listen with your ear
smell with your nose
touch with your hand
find a way in yourself or
turn to bones.

Jim Vanderbeek :: Grade 8
Oltman Junior High School :: St. Paul Park

. . . And the Poem Said . . .

The poet was writing a poem,
    But the poem was writing on its own.
The poet said, "Why do you take over like
    That?"
And the poem said nothing.

The poet was washing his face,
    But the poem jumped up on the sink.
The poet said, "Why do you bother me
    So?"
And the poem said nothing.

The poet was eating his dinner,
    But the poem was nowhere around.
The poet said, "Why do you hide like
    That?
And the poem said nothing.

The poem is a mysterious thing
    With answers to all questions.
But the poem is shy and will not speak for
    Itself.
The poem will say nothing.

Eva Curry :: Grade 4
Annunciation School :: Minneapolis

The Truth of a Stone

The truth of a stone
Is soaked in midnight thunder.
Granite crumbling into the sapphire
Skies of tomorrow.
The stories a stone might recite if
It were blood searing through
Our inner coals.
Spilling truth by twilight at a
Midnight ecstasy.
Excited lips tell everyone
The flaming dream
Lost in the night slumber.
The mist
the wind
the sun
the rain
the horse's mane,
The stone gazes over all.
No outbursts
Only calm serenity,
For the stone
Resonates in
Silence.

Barry Jesinoski :: Grade 12
Battle Lake School :: Battle Lake

The One Who Judges Jewels

From the rocky ledge I watch
the one who judges jewels as
he stands alone by the glassy green sea.
The salty breeze tugs
at his long hair
and ruffles his worn dungarees.
His spectacle-rimmed eyes
examine the brilliant gems.
He inspects each ruby, sapphire and diamond
with certain meticulousness
as they rest like marbles
in his large rough hand.
His reflective eyes
determine the worth of each stone
perhaps seeking a deeper value
hidden beneath the surface.
Sorrow flickers in his eyes.
I draw nearer and dare to inquire
"Why are you so sad?"
The one who judges jewels
welcomes my interference
and offers an explanation.
The answer that I request requires a journey
and the one who judges jewels
becomes my guide.
His large rough hand grasps mine
and we begin to climb.
He leads me away from the
glassy green sea
and into a dark moist cave-tunnel.
We emerge into a private garden
lush with emerald mosses and shrubs.
Delicate flowers climb
intricate vines
while butterflies

dance and frolic above.
The natural beauty surrounds us.
The secret paradise is priceless.
The one who judges jewels
reaches into his frayed pocket
and the gems that he had been studying
fall to the ground
to hide among the grasses.

Tammy Anderson :: Grade 12
Mankato East High School :: Mankato

LIFE

Life is like a little spaceship drifting
towards Pluto and hurtling back towards home base, Earth.

    Lucky that I don't run into the stars.
    Lucky the teacher doesn't hit me with a ruler.

Wait a minute, life is like a flower struggling to get its
seed planted in the ground.
It grows, then wilts.
Its seeds fall and start to grow.

    Luckily the bees don't come and shove you over.
    Luckily the gardener doesn't forget to water you.

Wait a minute?
Life is like dust that comes and goes.

    Lucky the housekeeper comes to wipe me away.

I am lucky!

    My life is simple and easy like the flower's.

Missy Lund :: Grade 5
Woodbury Middle School :: Woodbury

THE WIND SPIRITS

When the long winters
Were passing by
The fields were wet and muddy.
We liked to go to a rock pile.
The rocks were so many colors.
The rocks were by a little forest
With green and red trees.
A big green tree
Had a branch we called the door.
We would ask the Indians nervously
If we could come in
Then the wind would blow hard
If they didn't want us in
The wind wouldn't blow at all
If they wanted us in
We would have to give thanks
By giving pine cones or
Other beautiful things on this earth
When we would walk back
We would get mud in our little shoes
When we were back
We could feel their powerful spirits
With us every day and night
When we're in danger or down
We will always know we have
The Indians in our hearts to talk to.

Kari Spielman :: Grade 6
Balaton School :: Balaton

The True Meaning of Life

It was a bright day in a very spacious room. White walls, white floor, white ceiling. The sweet aroma of a warm summer day filled the air. She sat in the middle of the room, levitating about two feet above the floor in a circle of white candles, and all she did was meditate. The atmosphere was very pure.

"Hey!" Her meditation was interrupted.

She screamed.

"Don't worry, I'm just here to help," the voice said.

"Help what? Who are you? How did you get here?" she asked, as if in a confused state.

"None of that matters," replied the voice, who she could see was a man in a black robe.

"What?! If that doesn't matter, then what does?" she asked.

"Nothing. Just follow me," the man said, commandingly.

She stood up and followed him out of the room. When she walked out the door, her surroundings seemed different than usual. Instead of the normal hallway, there was a street where she saw the man at a window across the street.

She looked in the window, and asked, "Where are we? Who are they?"

The man calmly replied, "Look into the window. Can you not say who appears before your eyes?"

"Oh yes," she said, peering into the window, "That little girl looks like me, and that man is my father!"

"Oh no, he's not!" the man corrected.

"Who do you think you are?!" the woman demanded.

"Why, my lovely, I am the Ghost of Your Past," he said. "I know everything that ever happened in your life, as a result of what you've done.

"You see, when you were very little, about three or four weeks old, your mother and father put you in an orphanage. That man adopted you shortly after, and raised you as his own. He never told you that he was not your father, or even that you were adopted. He didn't want to see you cry. As he raised you, he taught you everything he knew. That is why you were levitating when you were meditating."

"I wasn't lev—wait! That's why my butt hurt when you interrupted me!"

"Exactly. And when you left your so-called 'father,' at 18, you depressed him; drove him into alcoholism. He died shortly after."

"Who do you think you are!?" the woman screamed. She closed her eyes and shouted, "Leave me alone! I don't want to see you ever again!"

When she opened her eyes, she was back in her room, alone. She sat down again in the middle of the circle of candles, assumed the meditation position, and started thinking deeply about what just happened.

"Wake up!" she heard after what seemed to be a couple of hours.

"She looked up and saw a man wearing a white robe. Surprised, she asked, "Who are you?"

"You need not worry about minor details, but if you insist, I will tell you. I am the Ghost of Your Present. I know everything that is happening as a result of your actions in life. Come with me, and I will show you."

"This is starting to remind me of that story 'A Christmas Carol'!" she said. And with that, she followed him out of the room. And again, it was not the normal hall. It was a balcony, a fire escape.

"This is the apartment down the hall from yours," the ghost explained. "They are playing, or trying to play, their favorite game. All they need is one more person."

"But they're not my type of friends, they're loud and obnoxious. I wouldn't think of associating with them."

"That is the impression they give *you*. Give them a chance, and I'm sure you can have a good friendship with them."

"But what—-", she looked back to talk to the ghost, but he was gone. She looked around, and saw her room. She decided to try meditating once more.

"Don't bother," a voice said as she was about to step into the ring of candles.

She turned and looked at the source of the voice and saw a man dressed in a psychedelic robe.

"Let me guess: the Ghost of My Future?" she guessed.

"Precisely. I know everything that'll happen in the future of your life, and today I'm gonna show you.

"Follow me, I'll take you where no man has gone before: to your future."

She followed him out of her room, and again, instead of the hallway, it was a convent with nuns walking by as if they didn't notice them. The ghost was standing at a large, locked door. She approached him.

"C'mon," he said, as he walked through the door.

"I can't walk through doors!"

"Believe me, you can now!" he said, and pulled her through.

On the other side of the door was an elderly woman in a straitjacket, looking as if she had seen all the gods from every religion all at once.

"Wh-who is that?"

"That, my friend, is you. Of course, that is if you keep going on the way you are now."

"What happened to me?"

"You went totally crazy trying to figure out the true meaning of life, instead of taking it day by day and for what it's worth."

"So all that meditating could be for the worse?" she said in an obvious state of confusion.

"Yeah! And if you don't stop trying to figure out what life really is, this is where you will end up.

"C'mon, let's go back to your place. This gets kinda depressing."

In a blink, she was back in her apartment with the last ghost.

"So what will happen to me if I stop all this heavy meditating and get a social life?" the woman asked curiously.

"No, no! I'm sorry, *that* I can't tell you. But what I can tell you is this: don't worry about the meaning of life and start worrying about the meaning of your social life."

When she looked up, he was gone, but she thought about what all three ghosts had said, and called her neighbors, getting back in the flow of things.

The moral of the story is: Try to correct mistakes you have made in the past, think about others now, and don't worry about what will happen in the future.

Travis Howard :: Grade 9
Rockford High School :: Rockford

The Perfect World

Scene opens with Liz sitting in a beach chair, relaxing.
It is night, and the moon and stars are out.
Music plays: slow soft flute music.
Liz's eyes slowly fall shut. She sleeps.
A sudden blast of ugly Saxophone music.
As the music plays, three people come from the shadows
and form themselves into a strange looking Jug.
One of them makes a strange squeaky noise, another
whispers "angle, angle, angle, angle . . ." The third
whispers "Circle, Circle, Circle . . ."

Liz opens her eyes, walks around the jug.

LIZ
What a strange looking Jug!

> The JUG people suddenly thrust out their arms and suck
> Liz into the Jug. She screams.

AHHHHHHHHHHHHHH!

> They swallow her into the jug, with loud, banging music
> playing under the scene.
> Silence.

> Guitar plays: soft, sweet, slow. The Jug people turn slowly
> and become trees. Two other actors walk slowly in, and
> raise their arms to become trees. The feeling is extremely
> calm and slow, like being in a beautiful dreamland. Liz
> rises, and walks through the trees.

LIZ
What beautiful trees. What glorious mountains. I feel safe here.

Liz walks behind the grove of trees, and they re-form into a tunnel with a door on it. Liz looks with curiosity at the tunnel structure. The actors who have formed the tunnel turn to her and say:

ACTORS
Gold Mine.

They go back to the tunnel form. The door of the gold mine (one of the actors) swings open, as the other actors provide the noise of creaky hinges. Two people come out of the gold mine. They look as if they might be people, or they might be spirits in human bodies.

Person 1
Hello Liz.

Person 2
Help Liz.

Person 1
What makes you sad?

LIZ
You live in this perfect world. Where I live nothing is perfect. Everybody sins, and nothing is right, everything is wrong.

(The two people from the gold mine go to her, put their hands on her head.)

Person 1 and 2
We have something for you.

(They go back to the gold mine.)

Person 1 and 2
We'll be right back.

(They disappear into the gold mine. They come back carrying a gift, wrapped. The actors playing the gold mine surround Liz along with the two spirit people. They circle around Liz, chanting.)

CIRCLE OF ACTORS
Use this in remembrance of the perfect world!

(Music builds under them as they circle and chant. All the spirit people disappear off stage. Music suddenly stops, with a big blast on the bass drum. Liz is back on the beach, the gift is in her hand. She opens the gift. It is a bar of gold.)

LIZ
This is more precious than gold from the earth. I realize now those people were real. Now I know I can live on the Earth and not sin.

Liz Hook :: Grade 6
Our Lady of the Lake :: Mound

Jumping off Cliffs at the Boundary Waters

All of us together
canoeing up the sparkling water
to the mountainous cliffs.
Songs of bravery overwhelm my senses
leaving me frightened to make any attempt.

Finally I make my way up the dirt path
hearing only the intimidating laughter of the cliff
pounding in my ears.
At the same time
my heart crying louder with each step
until I reach the top.

The songs of encouragement drown my heart's thumping.
At last I am overcome with confidence and bravery.

I jump! Swimming in the air, trying to hold on to nothing.
Splash! I am alone and laughing
overjoyed with my accomplishment.

I look upward to the sky
feel the sun's warmth congratulate me.
I was never afraid to jump
I was only afraid to try.

Nkoyo E. Iyamba :: Grade 12
Convent of the Visitation :: Mendota Heights

Stone vs. Heart

A stone that breaks people's hearts
It shall sink into people's hearts like a
submarine diving into great depths.
A heart is a place for the humble and
peaceful.
A place where either anger or happiness
hangs on.
A heart with strong love and feelings is a heart
made of gold.
Therefore no stone could break a heart
of a person made of gold.
Sorrow and unhappiness are anger's nickname
A heart that is made of glass.
An empty heart feeds off the anger you
build up.
A sense of uneasiness hangs from this
person.
A stone could devastate this heart of glass
unless it changes to a heart of happiness and love.

Rich Kirk :: Grade 8
Oltman Junior High School :: St. Paul Park

Self Portrait

I am a kid
who is tired,
unlike a dead animal
which owns unending sleep

Noises in my head
speak in different tongues —
one minute voices speaking weirdly,
then squawking like birds —

Every minute I change and change,
like soil, like water, like life.

Ryan Bigelow :: Grade 5
Lakeview Elementary School :: Robbinsdale

The Mystical Eye

What is that evil mirror absorbing your image?
What is that marble-like vacuum
that traps your reflection?

It's your evil eye, taking in the world
hour by hour, minute by minute, second by second—
the eye that has a giant door closing
out the rest of the world during the night.
But during the day the door opens
and the eye sets its mystical powers to work.

Like a rainbow with many blended colors
the eye is a large TV screen—
it's like Zubaz, wild and crazy.

So beware! The eye may unleash
its hypnotizing powers on you
and take you into its own dimension—
or the Hoover Vacuum may suck you in.

Ricky Sullivan and John Mitsch :: Grade 5
St. Rose of Lima School :: Roseville

The Sea Shell

The sea shell is a mysterious thing.
It is bumps on an old man's head
That has no growing limit.
You hear a fierce storm inside of it,
Wild winds rage around the bruised sea.
When the storm is over, the sea is as green as
The grass swaying in the wind.
Soon another storm comes in as fast as a
Speed boat goes around a pond four times.
Still it holds a secret like a safe that can't be opened.
Could it be a secret in the future
Or something that raged around millions of years ago
Like a sound maker just for human pleasure?

Scott Hella :: Grade 5
Lanesboro Public Schools :: Lanesboro

Tip-Toes of a Crescent Moon

I speak the phrases
of a chickadee.

I set the sun
and tip-toe up
the crescent moon
high above the earth.

I have multiplied
the souls of the good.

I have peeked into
the sadness and
the willow which cries.

I have untied the earth
and set it free
to roam about the
    galaxies.

Mara Segal :: Grade 5
Meadowbrook Elementary School :: Golden Valley

Moon

The moon rises over the water.
The howling-moon shines on the mountains.
Grandparents sit on the porch in creaking rockers
telling stories to the children.
The moon rises over the water.
The howling-moon shines on the mountain.
Ancient faces, like crumpled silk.
Faces, eyes who have seen life,
ears who have heard its sounds,
a mouth that has tasted of its treasure.
All these things light up,
and become the moon.
The old grandmother stops her tale and looks at
her own face reflected in the pale disc of the moon.
The moon rises over the water.
The howling-moon shines on the mountains.
Soon all will be dark.
The stars are out.
The moon sets in the celestial valley,
and so does Grandmother.

Hannah Blair
Lake Country School :: Minneapolis

My Brother Will Never Be a Farmer

MY LITTLE BROTHER

My brother has a little toy farm.
The crane works as if it were real.
He runs over the horse as if it were
a part of the road.
He hangs the sheep as if they were
a bale of hay being brought
to the top of the shed.
The cow is dropped from the roof
as if it were just a rock.
The pig as well.
So there's only one thing I'm going to say,
"My brother will never be a farmer."

Aaron Weckman :: Grade 4
Jordan Elementary School :: Jordan

My Sewing Sister

Here is my sister sewing. Her silver needle looks like a bird pecking on a tree. Her blanket looks like the gold of a rich kind. When she stands she says, "Here is my blanket that's like the gold of a rich king." And then she will sit back down and start sewing again.

John Kent :: Grade 3
North Elementary School :: St. Peter

River of Chocolate

My mom is a river of chocolate
flowing on my taste buds.

She picks green money and spends it
on me to help me through the time warp
I'm going through.

My mom pours intelligence into my brain
to help me with all the Martian work
I have to do.

She runs on the path of love
filling my heart with the joy of living.

She leads me through darkness finding
the path I must glide through.

She sees through my eyes,
recording everything I see.

My conscience is my mom telling me
what's right and wrong.

Brian Daniels :: Grade 4
Royal Oaks Elementary :: Woodbury

My Family is Like a Sports Car

My family is like a sports car.
My dad is the engine
    always revving and roaring.
My mom is the muffler
    always trying to quiet him down.
My brothers are the wheels
    always running around.
My sister's mouth is the door
    always opening and closing.
And I am the frame
    just along for the ride.

Sean Bauch :: Grade 7
Fred Moore Junior High School :: Anoka

All About Me

My name is a state
so different and mean
like the wind
rushing by like
waves crashing on
rocks like the fish
in a pond swimming
like the wind like
blue mixed with white
like the crying
of an elephant
the tears so big.

Virginia Laursen :: Grade 2
Madison Elementary School :: Anoka

Don't Pull a Brigit

Don't ask so many questions!
Be Short.
Be Sweet.
Don't pull a Brigit.
Who cares if you don't know
what's going on.
I'm sure you can wait till later.
Don't pull a Brigit!
They want me to,
amputate,
mutilate,
abbreviate,
and eliminate my questions,
BUT I WON'T!
Don't pull a Brigit.
All I want is a reason,
so don't
incriminate,
discriminate,
ruminate,
and manipulate.
It's not like I committed
Treason!
Why can't I pull a Brigit?
So if you want to be short and sweet.
Act dumb and you'll become the most
famous person in the room,
but I'll still pull a Brigit.

Brigit Riley :: Grade 8
Central Middle School :: Columbia Heights

Picture Puzzled

A photo is on the table.
I pick it up and see
That the children in the photo
Could never have been Sis and me.
It shows two children in a hall,
The girl three, the boy four.
They wear plastic sun glasses
As they stand near a door.
The girl's glasses are white fairy wings
Making cute her face.
His make him seem an alien
Come from outer space.
The worst part about the photo
Is that the kids seem to like each other.
Yet I do know that the picture
Is of my sister and me, her brother.
So it's impossible, this photo—
Sis and I are awful foes.
The picture is convincing,
But I think
     it's superimposed.

Adam Cerling :: Grade 7
Farmington Middle School :: Farmington

The Sting

"No, you can't play with us! This is a secret club, and you can't join!"

I was six years old and at my best friend Jessica's house. She had invited me over to swim, and while we were drying off, her big sister Heather and her best friend had draped an old worn blanket over the picnic table for a clubhouse.

Jessica's full mouth broke into a pout, and a few wet, silky strands of blond hair wisped down her face.

"Daddy, they won't let us join their club."

Amused lights danced in her father's eyes. I didn't see anything that was funny.

"Why don't you two start your own club? You can call it 'The Jetson Orbiter's Space Club.'"

We were really into space, and the Jetsons were our favorite. We loved the idea, so we went to my house in search of a suitable clubhouse. There was a small tin shed in back of our house that was fairly empty, and we decided that it would be much better than any old picnic table. Heather would be *so* jealous. Served 'em right for being such snobs!

After we had cleaned it out, we went inside and shut the door. It was really dark and musty, except for where sunbeams sifted in through small cracks, but we loved it. Just as we were getting ready to settle down, we discovered that we had visitors, and they weren't the friendly sort. A hornets' nest was lodged up in the corner.

I opened the door, and Jessica grabbed a box and dashed out after me. In the box were small, pink plastic balls, and we were so mad that we started throwing them at the hornets from a dangerously close distance.

You can probably guess what happened next. We both got stung, but the real sting lay in the fact that all of our fantasizing about Heather's jealousy was shattered like broken glass around our feet.

Served us right for being such snobs!

Azra Babar :: Grade 9
Willow River School :: Willow River

A Train Going East

The young woman's clear blue eyes focused on the incoming train. Behind her, the little depot in the small town of Highmore, South Dakota, was dotted with people. An old man slouched on a bench fast asleep, a newspaper clutched to his breast. A young mother was pulled along by a lively little boy sucking a peppermint stick, his excited young face sticky from the candy. The woman scarcely noticed this. She was leaving a town that held nothing for her. She was going to the town of Gibbon, located in Minnesota, the state in which she was born.

At nineteen, she was going to be a schoolteacher. She had tucked her teaching certificate inside her worn, brown, cardboard suitcase. Held together by a piece of twine, she hoped the suitcase would hold up through the trip. The hot wind blew the sand around like snow. Her dark hair whipped about her face. She wore her best dress. Like everything else, it was brown for the country was in a great drought.

She boarded the train and handed the conductor, who tipped his hat, her ticket. She found a seat and settled herself down for the long ride.

She looked out the window at the drifts of fine dirt piled up along a fence. The wind howled incessantly. Countless grasshoppers swarmed across the buildings, wreaking havoc as they devoured the paint and even portions of the buildings.

The train exhaled a trail of coal black smoke as it started away from the train station. The day was warm, but the woman shivered. "It's going to be okay, Zylpha," she told herself, the wings of a nervous butterfly fluttering against her rib cage.

She thought back over the last two years of her life. It never rained. The drought persisted and grew worse with each passing day. The wind blew continuously, picking up the soil from the hot scorched earth. The sun blazed unmercifully from a dark, murky sky. And then, the grasshoppers came, blotting out the sun completely as they flew in to swarm over everything in sight. Anything green and growing was soon devastated in their frenzied feeding. Zylpha's stomach growled angrily, and she lay a thin arm across it, quite used to the feeling.

In the spring, Zylpha and her family had labored to plant an area the size of one square city block with potatoes. Just last week, Zylpha dug and dug, but succeeded only in finding enough potatoes for supper. They were the size of quarters. She sharply recalled the sun stroke she had received from the ordeal. Hopefully, now with one less mouth to feed, Zylpha's family could eat better.

Basically, the only other foods they had were a little hominy or hulled corn cured with lye, beans, and a few eggs from the chickens that survived by eating the plentiful grasshoppers.

Zylpha drifted off to sleep thinking of the supper she had no money to buy. She snapped awake when the train jolted to a stop. "Gibbon, Minnesota!" the conductor cried, "All off for Gibbon!"

Zylpha stretched and stood up. She reached for her suitcase on the rack above. She stepped off the train. It pulled away, gradually becoming only a dot on the horizon. She watched until it disappeared, and there was nothing there but the rosy sky with the sun peeping over the edge of the earth. She turned away, ready to begin her new life.

"Zylpha Busse?" a man's voice called from somewhere nearby. "Is there a Zylpha Busse here?"

"I am Zylpha Busse," she answered looking around, not knowing where the voice came from.

A man and his wife rushed toward her, the man extending his hand in greeting.

"Hello!" he boomed. "I am William Spaude, and this is my wife Anna. You were sent word that you were to stay with us, correct?"

"Yes, I was," Zylpha answered, suddenly shy.

"I bet you are nervous," Anna guessed. "I know I was on my first teaching job."

"Well, yes, I am," Zylpha admitted.

"Don't worry!" William resounded. "Just show them who's

boss, and you'll get along fine! Let's get you to your new home."

Soon, Zylpha had settled into the routine of teaching her 19 students. It was good to see well-fed healthy children.

Zylpha never tired of looking out the classroom window at the patches of green grass on the lawns. Trees still had leaves on them. Grasshoppers did not descend on you the minute you set foot outside, and the air was not filled with grit and dust as it was back home.

One day, Zylpha noticed a battered, old truck parking in front of the school. The door opened, and three dirty children dressed in rags tumbled out. The fourth child was but a baby, crying feverishly in his mother's arms. The father stopped the engine and leaned wearily against the steering wheel. Zylpha felt compassion for them and went out to see what she could do for them.

She found out that they were from Nebraska and were victims of the 'Dust Bowl.' Having lost their farm, they were on their way to Pennsylvania where they had relatives. The father asked if they could park by the school for a couple of days because the baby was sick. Zylpha consented to their request. She told the children that they could play on the playground, and she gave them toys she had confiscated from the mischiefmakers of her class. Zylpha often wondered if the old truck had ever made it to Pennsylvania. She had escaped the bad times. Had they?

Zylpha's teaching duties kept her busy, but she managed to find time to direct the church choir. One of the young men in the choir soon caught her eye. Soon they were meeting under the old apple tree in front of the school, getting to know each other better. Their friendship blossomed into a lifelong commitment. Zylpha realized, that the day she took the train east, was the day her life changed forever.

" 'A Train Going East' is based on the life of my grandmother, Zylpha Busse Kramer. She told me of the hardships she faced as well as the good times she has had in her life. Her eyes lit up with her memories, she recalled spellbinding things that she had experienced long ago. Her life truly has been colorful, because she lived through the struggles that people faced in the early twentieth century that most people could never dream could occur."

The Author

Marni Kramer :: Grade 10
GFW High School :: Winthrop

My Uncle Barry

My uncle is very generous and neat. He also has some strict rules. When I went on a trip with him last summer, he was very worried about his car. He would say, "Jared, where are your fingers?" when my fingers were on the back window, and "Jared, where are your feet?" when my feet were on the seat. Barry is someone I can talk to about anything and he will listen. We talk about problems of the world and how we think they should be solved. We also talk about how we think the dinosaurs became extinct. He gets on my nerves sometimes about me being messy, but we work it out. He keeps an open mind on most all things and is kind and imaginative. He likes to tell riddles and tries never to give up on the answers to my riddles. He is basically nice company to have around and I like him.

My uncle likes certain sports like hiking, volleyball and tennis. He likes to keep a journal on everything. While we were on our trip, Barry would record everything anybody did on his tape recorder and later transfer it to a journal. It drove me a little crazy because every time we went into a different state, he would record that on his tape recorder. He also recorded everything we ate when we went to a restaurant. He took pictures of everything on the way, like historical signs and many pictures of the same scene. Most of the time he is busy on something. My uncle also likes to tease although I know he's not serious.

Jared Detloff :: Grade 5
Swanville Public School :: Swanville

Inside My Family

My family is Laotian. Everybody was born in Laos, except my three little brothers. They were born in Thailand.

My family is the one that really values our religion, Buddhism. Everything we do is based on our religion. Here are some examples. Younger people are not to call older people by name. If I see someone and he is about 25 years old and his name is Frank, I would not call him Frank but "brother Frank." It might sound funny the way you'd say it in English, but it is very polite in Laotian. Also, you must bend down low when walking by an elder person.

You must not touch an elder person's head especially when it is a girl touching an older boy's head or a woman touching a man's head which is never done because it is very sinful. Why it is sinful is that a Buddha shaves his head and it is so that the head of a guy is precious because a Buddha is a guy. Those are some of the values we have.

Rice is very precious in Laos because without rice there is hunger. It was said that rice is the only survival of humans in Laos.

What our family most values is that any child in the family who is grown must take care of his or her parents. The other important value is that people like to be treated equally whether poor or rich, because we used to be real poor—so much that even our cousins wouldn't look at us or wouldn't help us a bit. If we needed food or anything, we were treated, shall I say, like we didn't exist in their path. But now that everything is going great for my family they would try to drive us and be nice to us.

Fong Inthavixay :: Grade 9
Worthington Junior High School :: Worthington

David

You stand, gently leaning on the brightly colored juke box, and watch as your friends start another game of pool. The colored balls breaking in different directions remind you of people running in fear, running from death. These thoughts of war are all that ever fill your mind—the idea of being drafted, the hope of the war soon ending, and the prayer that God will have mercy. The sound of the cue ball hitting the eight ball reminds you of gunshots. These thoughts won't stop. It isn't fair. You are a senior and you have no future plans. The only thing you or anyone else can concentrate on is this stupid war, which has no purpose. Suddenly your friends give you the signal that they are leaving. As you walk out the door you silently say goodbye to all the others in the 'Q.' You wonder, as you watch them goof around in their $2.00 haircuts, if they too are really worrying about their fates. As you finally let the door close behind you, you wonder if you'll see them Monday. Or, if you will ever see them again.

I had never met David before, and I was nervous about it all. When we finally met, all my anxieties were swept away. The first thing I noticed about him was his smile. It was so friendly, and it kept inviting my thoughts to flow. He seemed to be so content. It was hard to believe that at one time he had no idea what he wanted to do with his life. In the space designated for future plans under his senior picture, "unknown" was written. So it was for a vast number of other students. He enlisted and was sent to Germany. After returning, he finally became an engineering technician. He also became a very dedicated family man, something he was not during his high school years. David regrets rebelling and not talking to his parents more. He gave me good advice which I will carry with me for a long time. He told me to "Get to know your relatives, try to understand your folks, and talk to your grandparents. You'll learn a lot, and it will make your life much fuller."

You're wearing a pair of pressed dress pants, a long sleeved shirt, and some nice shoes. As you're walking through a knee-high pile of leaves you see your friends and run to catch up. They are dressed similarly and probably got their outfits at Brothers. As you open the door to the school, you watch two girls run by in knee-length skirts. The school day drags on, as it always does on Fridays, and you can't keep your mind on your books. Thoughts of girls, parties, and the everlasting thoughts of war race through your mind. Today you learned another friend had shipped out and thanked God that you hadn't had your eighteenth birthday yet.

Finally school is out and you are ready to cruise at seven. Your attire has changed into a more relaxed jeans-and-T-shirt look. Gas is cheap, 15 to 17 cents a gallon, depending upon the gas war with Blue Earth, so you spend a while checking out the strip. The radio is blaring while you drink your ten cent bottle of coke. The night has shown no real excitement—except a drag race. But that's normal, so you decide to go home. Tomorrow you'll meet the guys at the Sweet Shop for a cherry coke and fries. Now, however, you'll go to bed and dream about tomorrow night's big street dance, the moon landing, and about your future.

Teenage life was pretty much the same in the '60s as it is now. There is one major difference, and that is everyone's future plans. I feel sorry for all the families of the people whose lives were taken in the war; I never really knew how badly it affected those who were not in Vietnam. One thing I find amazing is that it only cost $57 for David to be born and $2,000 for me, 25 years later. Life 40 years ago doesn't seem too different, but I think I'll stay here in the '90s.

Teri Firkins :: Grade 9
Fairmont High School :: Fairmont

Brat

One day I was coming home from school and I ran into my little sister, Niambi. She looked sort of nervous and I asked her what was wrong. She said nothing was wrong, but held her coat tighter. When we arrived home she ran upstairs without taking her coat off. I followed her and when she got to her room she took off her coat.

Ahh-ha! She had on my shirt. That's why she had been holding her coat like that.

I stormed into her room and asked her why she took my shirt without asking. She said, "Because I wanted to." The worst thing about it is that the shirt was too big for her so she tied it in a knot. Now it was wrinkled at the bottom, and she also spilled Hawaiian punch on it. I was so upset, I wanted to slap her, but I kept my cool. I told her to wash my shirt, iron it, and return it the way it was or I was going to tell Dad.

She said "I don't have to. I'm Daddy's little Gemini."

I told my parents anyway, and they did make her wash my shirt.

Nkenge Ayoka Shakir :: Grade 8
Benjamin E. Mays School :: St. Paul

Days of Our Lives

I woke up one morning to the smell of fresh baked cookies. I got out of bed and went downstairs. My sister Sarah was in the kitchen baking cookies. She said they were for the bake sale.

I left the kitchen and turned on the T.V. I pretended to be watching it so I could see where she hid them. She would leave soon to get some more ingredients.

When I heard the door shut, I turned off the T.V. and went into the kitchen. I ate all the cookies but one.

Sarah returned home at 3:00, my mom would be home at 4:00. That would give me time to sneak out.

A door opened and closed with a bang. This time it was my mom. She was home early.

My sister was telling what happened when I came downstairs. Since there was no one else home, I had no one to blame it on. I said I was sorry and was assigned the exciting job of baking cookies and doing dishes.

Michael Spencer :: Grade 7
Benjamin E. Mays School :: St. Paul

A Lesson from Grandmom

My grandmom often tells me of the many conflicts and problems she faces on her job. She works mostly with white people. A lot of them do not like her because she is black. Not only because she is black, but also because she is a confident black woman who takes care of herself and dresses well.

They wonder how she can afford nice, expensive clothes and jewelry or even a nice sophisticated car. Simple! She works hard and takes care of herself and her things.

People often talk about my grandmom and isolate her on her job, but that doesn't bother her. If it did, she wouldn't be the person she is today.

"Always walk with your head held high. You can do or be anything you set your mind to. Don't let people put you down," is what she says to me.

I am glad my grandmom doesn't let those situations at work get her down. It takes courage to act the way you believe.

I can live by what she says because she doesn't fight back with her fists, but with a positive attitude and respect for herself.

Jessica McKinley :: Grade 8
Benjamin E. Mays School :: St. Paul

The Race

As each drop of water dropped slowly down her body Jenny became more and more nervous. The tension was unbearable. She never ever thought she could get this nervous at a swim meet. Of course this was the Junior Olympics, even so, she was so nervous that she felt as if someone was churning butter in her stomach.

The area was filled with talking and cheering but she didn't hear it. The smell of chlorine was awful, and she didn't smell it. There were people running back and forth in front of her, she didn't see it. All she could concentrate on was one thing. This one thing meant so much to her that it took her entire inner being and set it upon that one thing. It made her so nervous. Nervous like she had never been before.

The worst part of it was that she couldn't control her nervousness. She felt so sick. Would she ever be without this awful feeling in her stomach? Jenny felt scared, glad and miserable all at the same time.

This one thing was the water. In order to win this race she would have to beat it. She would have to make sure that she could swim right through it without a lot of trouble.

As she looked at it, she could see it smirking and smiling as it knew that she could not defeat it. It was shining blue and almost glowing. It was holding up the lane lines so proud and strong.

She was thinking to herself, most people don't know that a swim race is not only a race against the other people but also against the water.

As they called up her race all she could do was study the water. She was in a trance. She stayed in that trance until her swim coach tapped her on the shoulder. He gave her a couple words of encouragement and then proceeded to the side of the pool.

Jenny stood up on her block, bent over wiggling her arms and legs up and down. This movement helped to calm her down, but not enough to make her feel as good as she would feel when this was over.

She tried to block out the memory of past races and how hard her race, the two-hundred yard butterfly, was going to be. Only a few at her age could even finish, let alone finish fast. She could do it, she just kept telling herself.

The starter shot his gun, and she was off. Her first thought as she entered the water was, here we go. The water was cold, yet refreshing as she pulled and kicked through it. She was doing great, and she wasn't tired yet. She knew that if she just kept going like this, she would do fine.

The nasty water was no object to her now because she had not yet begun to tire. She was beating it, she was swimming right through it like a missile gliding through the air.

But this wonderful feeling lasted only through four lengths, and it was then that she felt like she was starting to slow down and the water was starting to gain control. No, no, she couldn't let it do that to her, she thought, so she pushed and pushed. Making every motion exactly in synchronization with the next. She was pushing so hard that every muscle ached and she could feel her heart beating so hard and fast that she almost thought it would beat right out of her body.

Jenny was really tired now but she wouldn't let herself think about that, she had to keep focused on this water. She had to work harder and harder to beat it now. Why was it doing this to her? She wished that it could just back down and let her win.

All this time she didn't even think to look at how she was doing compared to the others. Even if she had remembered, she probably wouldn't have looked because she didn't want to make one false move that would give the water an extra step ahead.

As she headed into her last turn she was so tired that it seemed that even though she was violently moving her arms she still couldn't obtain the speed she wanted. This last length was the most important. This was the length that you had to take all of the rest of your strength and go "all out." She had seen many people in last place catch up to second or third on the last length. She could do it.

She could barely move anything anymore. Everything was like jelly. She was having trouble breathing and she started to sink in the water. What was happening to her? Come on let's go, she kept telling herself, but nothing would work, until she took hold of all her feelings.

She figured out that she was holding back just a little bit so that she could survive the rest of the day, and so that she could make it out of the pool. But she also stepped outside herself and saw that she would survive if she used up the little bit of energy she had been saving.

That was all she needed. She took that little bit of energy and used it. She could feel the water backing down and just as she got to her utmost speed, her hand touched the wall and she stopped swimming.

She couldn't believe it. She stood up, not even realizing that she was done. She looked back at the pool and saw red, blue, and green caps, everyone of them behind her. She won, she had beat them all. She had beat the swimmers, the bad feelings, and the water. But the most refreshing thought was that she was done. Her tiredness and soreness didn't matter, she had beat everyone and everything, and it was all over now. She now knew what people meant when they said you can do anything if you put your mind to it.

Liz Goodman :: Grade 7
Blake Middle School :: Hopkins

The Old One

Your name smells like a farm
with dirt and gravel
because that's where you live.
Your name is driving
your old,
cigar-smelling pick-up.
Your name rides horses,
first bucking, then calm
because you are gentle.
Your name is fat and chubby
just like your waist.
Your name is like grandma,
somewhat gray and old
but very patient.
Your name is a slide,
sliding down
then starting again.
Your name teases me,
even in my mind.
Your name loves me,
and I love it right back.

Christy Boraas :: Grade 6
Madison Elementary School :: Madison

GRANDPA

Brown, red, and black plaid shirt
Farm magazine with creased pages
Newspapers stacked beside brown recliner
Grease on blue jeans that won't come out
Pliers in a holster on his belt
Jackknife in right pocket
Wallet in back pocket
Big silver belt buckle
A western movie on TV
Three-wheeler going through mud
John Deere 4020 tractor working hard
Cup of coffee and toast
Orange vest for hunting deer
Front page of the Star Tribune
John Deere cap fading
Las Vegas casino pen
Las Vegas card with a hole in the middle
Picture window watching for deer
Pete, the dog—"don't jump"
Boots with mud leaving tracks on the sidewalk

Aaron Peter :: Grade 6
Elmore Elementary School :: Elmore

Sewing As Fast As a Car

This is my grandma
Sewing me a dress,
Real fast, as fast as a three-wheeler
In fifth gear.
She's sewing on the collar
Of my dress and finishes like a cat climbing up a tree when
a dog is after it.

When I try it on, it feels like
Grandma's hugging me.
When I go home that day
I feel like wearing it every day.

Kelsey Olson :: Grade 4
Appleton Elementary School :: Appleton

SERENITY

My Uncle Henry,
Dad's brother-in-law.
Gone now, so serene.

As was his house, in
Bloomington, Minnesota.
Only a few blocks off
two major freeways,
but so serene.

A jet overhead, a trail
of white. A cuckoo
clock, with whistle broken,
clicks in the new hour.

And now dinner, with Aunt
Mildred. Unusual smells, but
each meal a winner.
Rhubarb was always
a favorite, dinner was
serene.

And Henry's pills at dinner-time.
Orange, light-blue, red-and-white.
Eight or nine at a time. Taking
the pills took more time than eating
dinner.

And after Mom and Mildred
washed the dishes, we would
slowly lumber down into the
basement. TV or "UNO."
Calm and serene.

The landscape, the interiors,
all the happenings, so
serene for the metro place.

It seems, there was
not much change for
Henry when he died.
So serene.

That's nice to know.

Orin Johnson :: Grade 11
RTR High School :: Tyler

A Mingling

What Is It?

What is a poem?
A poem is an outside world.
It's a lonely forest, creator of words.
A poem is news, an eagle, a peaceful lake,
It's a silent swan, rustling leaves,
eye-catching, knowledge,
a hooting owl.

What is poetry?
Poetry is outer space, a lonely alley,
a variety of words.
Poetry is music, a dream,
a spaceship to far off places.
It's a new beginning, the floating air,
a magical world, the country.

What is a poem?
A poem is a silent tiger sneaking up on its prey.
It's a car driving through your brain,
handing out ideas.
A way of talking, writing down your thoughts,
bouncing hair, lights,
and the cool midnight air.

What is a poem?
A poem is a marathon man,
dangling earrings, a smiling person.

What is poetry?
Poetry is a sharp car, a modern thought,
and sparkling teeth.

What is a poem?
A poem is clothes matching, a free bird,
an open door.
It's a worldwide brain, electronic thoughts,
outer space, and a bunch of glamorous words.

Cindy Skogerbor :: Grade 4
Sand Creek Elementary School :: Coon Rapids

BE A GOOD POEM

Be a good poem
Be interesting
Be fluent
Don't be rhyming

Be a beautiful poem
Be descriptive
Be vivid
Don't be vile

Be a long poem
Be full of words
Be writing big
Don't be paragraphy

Be a repetitious poem
Be using "be" every line
Be annoying
Don't be boring

Be a poem Ms. Burress likes
Be benevolent
Be giving me an "A"
Just be a good poem.

Lori DeLaitsch :: Grade 8
Central Middle School :: Columbia Heights

A Mingling

I strolled.
An occasional sea spray,
powdery white sand mingled with wind & water,
I became one with the scape,
danced on the line between surf and sand.
Further out I skipped,
glints off the water, a stirring inside me, I leapt,
let go of my self.
Up with me rose the silvery creatures,
the harmony of surf & wind joined with my spirit,
two dolphins dancing with me,
all colors and feelings released, effervescence—
A wave rolled,
closed in and washed me over, made my skin glitter.
The dolphins dove.
I watched.
They took part of me and left parts of themselves.

Dee Dee Budde :: Grade 8
Central Middle School :: Columbia Heights

The Mississippi

The Turquoise
   water crashing
     up against the
      rocks like a
        knife slicing
       an apple in
         half. An eagle
       flying above
     me with
    golden wings
   spread apart
and talons
shining in the
sunlight. Sailboats
sailing down the
  river as if there
    were a hand just
     pushing them
      along. What
     a gleaming
      sight it is!

Tracey Muralt :: Grade 5
Elm Creek School :: Maple Grove

OLD MISSISSIPPI RIVER SONGS

Splash Splash
the river splashes against the rocks
Swooh Swooh
the rain hits the water
Bang Bang
the lightning hits the river
Pow Pow
the old Mississippi bangs
bangs bangs on the rotten logs
Sha Sha Sha
the young beaver bites
down the trees
Rustle Rustle Rustle
the young trees hit the water
Shiss Shiss Shiss
the old Mississippi rolling
rolling rolling down stream
Wissle Wissle Wissle
the wind blows on the river
Sh Sh Sh
It's me listening
to all the noise
from the old Mississippi.

Missy Mollick :: Grade 4
Kennedy Elementary :: Hastings

Pop, Pop, Crunch, Crunch

When my dad turns the crank
for popping popcorn,
it sounds like tin clanking together
on empty streets at night.
    POP, POP, POP

It looks as though he's
on a ten speed bike
in tenth gear pumping for his life.
    Pump, Pump, Pump

The steam coming from the popcorn popper
is so hot it feels
like it will lift a hot air balloon.

But when he's all through,
I smell his buttery popcorn.
I feel as though I could
eat it all in one second.

And once I taste it,
I can't stop eating it!
    Crunch, Crunch, Crunch

Matthew P. Borg :: Grade 4
Lincoln Elementary School :: Fairmont

Kitchen Songs

Bark Bark go
the dogs next
door who will
never be quiet
CklCkl goes
the bacon
on the frying pan
Rachel! Get
me a Kleenex says
my sister when she
is a foot away from it
and I am upstairs
Come set the table
says my mom
Tap Tap Tap go
the forks, spoons
and knives MMM
says my dad

Rachel Breitenbach :: Grade 2
Winston Churchill Elementary School :: Rochester

Low B-Flat

When I first opened,
    the gray case,
    the smell of slide oil,
    touched my nose.
The shiny brass,
    gleamed,
    under fluorescent lights.
The mouth piece,
    shined,
    silvery,
    against the black lining.
My own reflection,
    stared back,
    at me.
Then,
    I got to assemble it.
Putting,
    the glimmering brass,
    pieces together.
Placing,
    the silver mouth piece,
    into the end.
Locking,
    and unlocking,
    the slide.
Holding it,
    the right way.
Feeling proud,
    of myself.
Blowing,
    getting,
    a low sound.
Trying,
    other positions,
    with my shaky hands.

Moving the slide,
> up,
> and down.

Feeling,
> the easy movement.

Disassemble,
> putting,
> each piece,
> back,
> in the proper places.

Again,
> glancing,
> at the beauty,
> before,
> closing the case,
> to take,
> my,
> school-rented,
> trombone,
> home,
> for the first,
> time.

Jennifer Wetherbee :: Grade 6
Oak Grove Intermediate School :: Bloomington

Flowers Around Me

I am at my ballet recital.
I can feel the floor almost
gliding me across.
The floor is a smooth
sheet of clear glass.
I can hear the ballet music,
soft like a canary
singing me to sleep
at dusk.

Here I am in a long pink tutu
like a pink flower
wrapped around me
with shiny sequins
sewn on it.
It looks like stars
glittering in the dark
night sky.

The stage is filled with the leathery
smell of ballet slippers,
along with the smell of sweat
like a hot summer day.

The sparkling lights
shine on my face
like hot fire.
The thunderous applause
pleases me very much.

Rachel Squires :: Grade 5
Woodbury Middle School :: Woodbury

The Telephone

A telephone is the way people get
into a new world. Even if it's on the other side
of the earth. One telephone will take you
to heaven, the other will take you to Mars.
There are dark tunnels in the numbers
of the telephone. The telephone
has a dark side and a light side.
The dark side has fire breathing
bunnies in it. The light side has
tame foxes. You can never
feel its teeth biting into your ear.

Magenta Miller :: Grade 3
Northrop Montessori School :: Minneapolis

A Little Anger Sometimes

I don't have a lot of courage
just a little anger sometimes
when people put me down or yell
when I feel maybe
I can't go on anymore
when I do something wrong
take something out on someone else

I tell my brothers to just leave
me alone
I'll try to solve it myself
But if I can't, I got friends to rely on

John Poegel :: Grade 10
Swanville Public School :: Swanville

Call It Selective Hearing

"Rue! Rue Ann! You left my glasses in Atlanta!" yells George. George is always telling me I do everything wrong.

"George dear. I'm sorry." Oh my. George has that look on his face again.

"Rue! Why I tolerate you is beyond me! First, you left my best golf club on the ferry after we crossed the Mississippi at New Orleans. Then my best underwear got abandoned at a hotel in Orlando. My Penguin tie is now somewhere in Washington D.C. in a taxicab. Now my sunglasses are who knows where in Atlanta! For goodness sake, Rue. I need some clothes left when we get back to Montana."

"What did you say dear?" I don't even listen to his rants any more. Call it selective hearing if you must. I call it not going deaf.

"Dear! You don't even hear what I say! Goodness sakes."

Ahhhaa. He's shaking his head, now he's walking off to grumble in peace. That means peace for me too. Ouch! I seem to have forgotten to put any suntan lotion on. Back to George in the cabin. This Caribbean cruise is lovely.

"Lady! For the seventh time in five seconds. THE SHIP IS SINKING!"

Oh dear. Lifeboats left I hope.

"Lady! Quit yawning and shrugging and move that body!"

Sheesh. That cabin boy needs more exercise. He looks like a hippopotamus.

"Move it now!"

I'm moving! I'm moving! You act like the boat is sinking." What a stubborn boy.

"But it is sinking!"

Hmmmm. Funny, I wonder why he fainted.

Natalie White :: Grade 5
Elton Hills Elementary School :: Rochester

Chapter Two: The Fortune Cookie

Oh, what's that over there? Is it what I think it is. It is! It's a pot of gold! Now what could I do with it? I know, I could go out to eat, at a place that is real nice.

Now that I'm here I will order some rice and chicken. Oh, that was good. I think I'm ready for my fortune cookie now. I'll see what my fortune says. It says, *"In the future you will be robbed."* Oh, who believes in that junk? I'll go home now. I'll go check on my gold now. OH, NO, IT'S GONE! My fortune was right. I never did believe those things till now. Now I have a real case to solve. Where should I start looking? I know what I should do, I should follow their foot prints in the snow. I better get started before it gets dark.

Makalah Haessler :: Grade 3
Castle Elementary School :: Oakdale

The Brazil Nut with Nine Faces

My Brazil nut is like a brown old leaf
that has just fallen from a maple tree in the fall.
It vibrates like a thousand springs
jumping up and down.

Its ridges bob up and down
like driftwood
on a cold, windy day.

It looks like an old, rusty Holland shoe,
all rusty and gray.
It looks like a mountain ridge, with dirty black snow.
It rocks like a rocking chair, bobbing up and down.

The nut is like an old, brown, broken-down boat from a
violent storm below.
It smells like old black smoke
from a fire burning bright
It looks like an old black ship
with the captain ready to turn off the light.

Andrew Burth :: Grade 4
Newport Elementary School :: Newport

The Hand

Hey Hand, you're not
as dainty as a snowflake.
You starfish
with no mouth.
Hand, a cactus with
no points.
Get me in trouble
why you made me steal a cookie.
What about my scar?
You made me do that too.
You help me swim,
How do you do it?
Dirt, more and more dirt.
Painting, what about that?
You know I can't paint.
What about my finger-
nails? They're certainly not round,
I can't believe that you
can help me catch a ball.
Hand as beautiful as peacock feather,
Hand you are the most
wonderful thing.

Dan Compton :: Grade 4
Deerwood Elementary School :: Eagan

Hands

Like rings in a mighty oak,
lines on one's hands
show past experiences and adventures
the indentations in the bark
are like the very pores in our skin
they show all our triumphs
and even our defeats.
The scars
show all the difficulties
and hard work.
showing your hands to a stranger
is very much
like an introduction.

Dan Schwarz :: Grade 7
LeSueur Junior High School :: LeSueur

Blessed

I am a picture
without any words
I am as enthusiastic
as a spiritual leader
I am as blessed
as a baptized baby
I am an expeditionist
like a fish
I am a rebel
without an attitude
I am a cliche
in society's eye
I am a finger
pointing the way.

Michelle Gilbert :: Grade 12
Guadalupe Area Project :: St. Paul

LITTLE DIPPER

Little Dipper, I don't think
you're a little dipper,
you're a pot. You boil
a lot of hot water.
Pot, you scoop up
all the happiness and pour
it out on me.

Sotearit Chak :: Grade 4
Cherokee Heights Elementary School :: St. Paul

Cassiopeia

Cassiopeia, you don't look
like a queen. You look like
two mountains standing
side by side in space
with no cares in the world.

Stacy Reed :: Grade 4
Cherokee Heights Elementary School :: St. Paul

BIG DIPPER

A busy scooper
full of ice cream
scooping up the stars
all day
all night

Minne Vang :: Grade 4
Cherokee Heights Elementary School :: St. Paul

ORION

You're not Orion.
You're just a butterfly,
floating in the sky,
like a drifting leaf,
floating from the sky.

Nina Raulerson :: Grade 4
Cherokee Heights Elementary School :: St. Paul

Along with My Mind

The eraser is like a broom
sweeping away the dirt.
When it goes across the blackboard
it takes away the words
along with my mind.
When the words are off the board
my mind is blank.
I think of nothing.
The eraser is black as night —
no stars, no moon.
The board is like the night, too,
with its dark black sinking
into my mind, making it blank.
There is no moon, stars,
no planets, for the eraser
has made the board blank
along with my mind.
As smooth as a baby's skin
the eraser sways along the board
like a tree in the wind,
a blade of grass, a person's hair.
When it runs along the board
it takes the words off
and my mind away.

Nancy Kadlec :: Grade 8
McGregor School :: McGregor

My Club House

My club house is a dragon
that breathes fire.

My club house is a jungle.

It is an enemy shelter.
And the colonel says to move in.

It is a ship moving into place.

It has an escape roof.
It is white and red.

What a club house!

Shayne B. Meyer :: Grade 3
Sandstone Elementary School :: Sandstone

Dear Lake

How do you move?
How do boats float
on you? Do you go down
in the earth or are you a hole
with water? Do you
have friends? Do you like
fish? Do you like boats?
How do boats float on you?
I like fishing on you.
Why do you have blue
clothes? Do you like swimming?

Clayton Engen :: Grade 1
Aquila Primary Center :: St. Louis Park

It Flies with Feathers

Gold Sparrow

Gold sparrow wings wide crawling to the sky.
Black ashes bring taste to the ground in my face.
Collapsing hail, chase the snow into the
frightened rain. My head glows
like an apple on a small tree.

I sing to you in the trees.
I retrieve a bone in my dream.
Weeping willow at nine. The sun that
brought forth me erupted. When will
you touch my soul?
You left without telling
me if the sky ends.

Eric Andrews :: Grade 7
Oltman Junior High School :: St. Paul Park

The Sign of the Dove

It was open to earth from
the whiteness of the clouds and
the welcoming from above.

It flies with feathers
as white as snow. It's as big
as a glass slipper trying to
become known. Its eyes like
the shining of a lake in
autumn mourn.

It's as old as no tomorrow.

As it flies by it sounds
like whispers in the wind

The dove's beauty gives
the sunset a treasure of life
and a rose more color, beauty
and strength to hold up
during God's power.

The dove's hunger is
as big as the morning dawn.

The dove is the sign that helps
us cherish life.

Carolyn Hudalla :: Grade 7
Oltman Junior High School :: St. Paul Park

Birds of Prey

I used to walk along the sky
with the birds of prey.
I used to fly alone with me.
I used to hear the sound of
a midnight hawk,
mixed with the roar of an eagle.
I used to hear the hoot of an owl,
Hoo hoo,
hear him calling out to me,
and hear the rustling leaves
after a blow from a hard wind
or the great swoop of a heavy raven.
I used to hear the wail of an eagle
above a moonstruck earth,
and hear the movement of a feather
after a smooth takeoff.
I used to hear the click of a claw
after the catch of a fish,
and hear the screaming wind of
the mountain,
on the feather that streamed through it.
I used to hear the lift of every feather
and the push of wind.
I used to hear the sleek wind,
when the bird shoots through like an arrow,
and hear the snap of a branch
when an eagle lands on a tree.
I used to walk along the shores
with the birds of prey.

Tony Housey :: Grade 7
Woodland Junior High School :: Duluth

PANTHER

At the beginning of time
before the sun burst bright
the darkness prowled.
When light came to reign
darkness left but a small trace behind.
Black as night,
eyes sharp as an eagle's,
cunning, and crafty as evil darkness,
the mighty beast rose . . .
Ruler of night.

Sparkling jewels, his eyes are.
Steel traps be his jaws.
His ears, like satellite disks
picking up sound.
His fur like great shadows
spreading darkness around.

His claws can tear the earth apart.
His teeth could crush an elephant's bones.
His strength, his power, is endless.

A spitting hiss crawls up his throat
as angrier he gets.
Then he stops,
silent as the wind blowing through his fur.

Hunger creeps upon him quickly,
quietly, cunningly, like a hunter stalking his prey.
He craves for food
as a miner wants for gold.
He angers, he raves
until, at last, he eats.

Dark as night, he quietly creeps upon his prey.
Fearless, unknowing, the prey, it is
until too late.
The hunter leaps into the air,
landing on an unsuspecting victim.
Victory, glorious victory!
The mighty hunter rejoices, and devours its prey.
The night has won.

The green world towers above him.
Beauty springs up everywhere.
Moss coats his path.
Trees shield his head.
Plants supply his prey.
For he, he is a majestic beast,
ruling powerfully,
proudly,
forever.

Mychal Lynn Anderson :: Grade 5
Glen Lake Elementary School :: Glen Lake

Reflections on a Summer Afternoon

and lo
songbirds play
the sun frolics
with the leaves

soft breeze
filled with
dust from
freshly-mown grass
has a chat with
the trees

dandelions debate
with the lilacs
about
various things

the cat sits nearby
listening intently
occasionally
offering her opinion

shouts
laughter
fill the air
as the call goes out
someone is going swimming
everyone else follows
as if reminded
of the heat

The clouds stop
to watch
as the stream dances
about
the sunning rocks

and so goes
a lazy
summer afternoon

Naomi Priscilla Smith :: Grade 8
Benjamin E. Mays School :: St. Paul

If I Were an Eagle

If I were an eagle I'd fly high above
my wings pushing against the wind
my wings are flapping slowly
upward and downward
When I soar, I leave marks
showing my beautiful brownish red
feathers
When I turn, I raise my right wing
and lower my left
I'm going down for lunch now
I circle the lake looking for my prey
I go down looking like a shooting star
I glare at the fish and grab it with both feet
my claws go into him
I have lunch, tear him up, eat him
and get filled

Tamara Eagle :: Grade 8
Heart of the Earth Survival School :: Minneapolis

A Streak of Beauty

The vast moon
of breaking old rock
sneaks through the black lifeless sky.
The doom that is always dreaded
is coming in the form of a hound.
The effervescent river
is the only savior
but also the only risk.
The racoon is cursed
to this cruel world
by the sly fast going wind.
His tail
as ringed as the last drop of water
from a rainstorm
falling into the biggest
puddle of color.
His teeth and claws
as long and sharp
as a saber toothed tiger's fangs.
Its fur as soft as a silk pillow
with tears of the gods.
The racoon's squeak
is as high as tinfoil crumpling
and it's as silent as the clouds.
The racoon's age
is as young
as the puff of fog
from your breath.
His hunger
as small as a grain of sand.

His speed
as fast as a cheetah powered
time machine.
He is the time
that stops time.

Aaron Morrison :: Grade 5
Katherine Curren Elementary School :: Hopkins

The Butterfly

Once upon a time there was a kid who loved butterflies. He had butterfly wallpaper, bedspread, shades, door and a stereo. Now you can see how much he loved butterflies. One time he went to a meadow. Do you know what he saw? He saw a dead butterfly lying on a limb of a tree. Now he was so mad. No one would even go by him. Not even the toughest kid could stop him. Anyone who would even touch a butterfly he would hit. Believe me, you would be in the hospital like that. When he went back to the place where the butterfly died, it was not there. He looked everywhere. He could not find it. All he saw was a little egg where the butterfly was. The butterfly had laid eggs. This kid was so happy he kissed the whole class the next morning. From then on he always went back to the meadow to see how the eggs were doing. Some of his classmates came with. The mom came back to see it too. It hatched 2 days later.

Jeremy Stewart :: Grade 3
Hillside Elementary School :: Cottage Grove

The Deer Who Followed Me

When I feel sad,
I go to my secret place
back in time
with the Indian tribes.
Meet the Sioux
and the brown, yellow, orange
forest in fall.
I meet the deer
with horns like
big branches.
It follows me, but
I say, "Go away, deer.
Go away.
You belong in the wild
where the bluebirds
sing a happy song.
In the wild
is where you belong.
Go away, deer. Go away.
You don't belong
here with me.
Go into the forest
and don't come back
until I'm sad again."

Mark Gudmastad :: Grade 3
Central Elementary School :: Winona

My Friend

When I hear your name I think of us
playing in the wind, your hair blows,
the air picks up your hair in the wind
like a kite soaring in the air.
I speak to you and it makes me feel good.
I talk to you in the breeze of the earth,
your hair talks to me like the world earth.
As we talk in the wind
you make me feel like my hair is feathers
floating in the wind that soars in the
night cool breeze— I feel like my hair is soaring in the breeze.

Jennie Grundeen :: Grade 2
Shirley Hills Elementary School :: Mound

LOVE

When the moon dances
I dream of a feather
whisping across the passion
of a couple.
He wears the teal lock
combing our love,
while jealousy is bubbling
into a hurricane.
My heart is a deep purple
drizzling sleep of the exhaustion
of a heartbreak.
Midafternoon falls into evening
and a lost soul caresses my hand
asking for my love back.
I admit my flaring emotions
as aqua strands of hair
embroider together smothering
the fire.
We forgive and forget
giving our love to each other again.

Gina Jaszczak :: Grade 8
Oltman Junior High School :: St. Paul Park

Forever Dreams

My Imagination

In the darkness of my mind,
I was scared of the dangers lurking there.

The silence was like a nightmare.
I walked through halls of emptiness.

There I found my imagination—
the tool of creation, the master of my mind.

Soon scariness went away,
and curiosity came.

I stepped in cautiously,
and I saw ideas coming and going.

The fullness was like a busy city.

I saw my stories before I wrote them,
my dreams before I dreamed them.

It was like a continuous dream.

Nicole Kolashinski :: Grade 5
Woodbury Middle School :: Woodbury

Forever Dreams

She is flying through the deep black sky with freckles of white. Her long hair flies free and her smile is enormous. She is on her bed, kneeling at the end. She is six years old as the thirteen-year-old dreams on.

She passes by an angel and she watches the earth over her shoulder. She sees peace and love as blacks and whites shake hands, as the Jewish and Catholic children play together, as the old and the young hold hands. She wishes to stay forever.

Back home it is cruel. The bombs of death fall before her eyes. The color of camouflage runs through the yard.

She will stay in her dreams. She will not wake up. She floats down to her room and watches herself sleep.

Karen Gilbertson :: Grade 8
Mankato East Junior High School :: Mankato

My Hands Jump

At night my hands
jump because they dance.
They are known to all creatures.
They jump and plie and spin
so fast you hardly see them.
They jump into bushes and spin
around the twisted branches and use leaves for tutus.
The wind whistles a tune
and crickets sing songs
of beauty and boldness.
Their dancing slippers
of dried bean seeds begin
to wear thin
so they come home to bed
strip off their tutus
and dancing slippers
and drift off to sleep.

Deanne Kociemba :: Grade 4
Holdingford Elementary School :: Holdingford

Hand

My hand is a turkey gobbling
on a guitar, eating the strings
and making noises go far away
into the city. My hand wants
to jump off and run around
and become an astronaut
and be famous and live for
a long time. He wants to fly away
to a far away land where
he can have a life and be rich
and have fun fun fun and be
very happy, so happy he will
scream and yell and eat a lot
of food, and run and play.

Kevin Sieben :: Grade 3
Pinecrest Elementary School :: Hastings

Excerpts From: The Tic-Tac-Toe Aliens

Here I am, in California, ready for the rocket to launch off. I have enough food and clothes for a year. The countdown starts; five, four, three, two, one, zero. "BLAST OFF!" I am up in space looking for an unknown planet! I am wondering, what will I find? Who will I meet? None of the questions can be answered yet. I looked down, the earth looked like a tiny ball. I went to get something to eat. There was a lot to choose from. I finally decided on chicken. I squeezed it out of the tube and ate it. After I was finished, I looked out the window. I saw something far off in the distance. It was a mixture of fluorescent pink and fluorescent yellow. I made the rocket go faster. The shape got bigger and bigger. It was the shape of a tic-tac-toe board. I ran to the back of the rocket to get some binoculars. When I found them, I ran to the front of the rocket and looked out the window. I saw little things, the shape of O's and X's in the holes. I made the rocket slow down. I got on my spacesuit. The suit is silver and fluorescent blue. I made the rocket go faster again. After two hours I finally landed on the unknown planet. I started to get out, then I hesitated. Was I sure I wanted to do this? Did I really want to find out what was on the other side of the door? Of course I did! I was brave!

***

"Oh, I wish I had a Fairy Godmother!"

Then, POOF! An old woman appeared! She wore a beautiful dress and held a gold wand. "Can I help a young dudette in distress?" she asked.

"Yes, me," I answered. "My rocket is out of gas and I may never get home!"

She smiled. "Do not worry, my child, I am your fairy godmother. My name is Hope Helpington," she replied sweetly. "I can help. What do you need to get the rocket running again?"

"Fuel," I said in a shaky voice.

"Okay, your wish is granted!"

All of a sudden, the rocket went fast. The earth was right under the rocket. "Oh, thank you! Thank you, fairy godmother!"

Just then she hugged me and disappeared into thin air. . . .

***

Chaitra Wirta :: Grade 4
Weaver School :: Maplewood

The Search

Chapter 1 The Start

Hi, I'm a young girl in Hawaii. I am trying to find the unsolved mystery of Amelia Earhart, to fulfill her dream. This is what I'm bringing: a map, 200 pounds of food, water, medicine, money, parachutes, 15 months worth of clothes, a mini-washing machine, books, cat Kittsy, and my dog Sally. Am I missing anything? I will fly around the world and stop in every state. I will not leave anything uncovered. I have people at every stop to fill me up. But I am scared. In this adventure you'll be helping me. Thanks. I have thin, silky black hair. I am very skinny. My name is Tara. Let's go!

Chapter 2 My Problem

We were right over Austin, Texas, where there were farms and windmills and stuff. But there was a blizzard and lightning struck my propellor and it came off and crashed! I was scared and I screamed. I was stuck so I couldn't get my parachute and I could only steer! I was 300 feet off the ground and my dog and cat were scared too! My cat and dog came on my lap! We all screamed with horror for 30 seconds!

Chapter 3 The Blue Dream

I screamed and fell asleep. I guess it froze time because I didn't fall any more. I had this special dream. It seemed like Amelia's spirit saw me! She said, "Here is my plane and a map of my crashing spot. Follow it and you'll be Blessed."

In my dream I saw a little boy with a heart-shaped body. "My name is Mark Hartman! Land and I'll fly your plane, use mine. Then come back for your plane. But also keep mine. Land on the cloud."

"O.K., whatever." Then I woke up! And did what my dream said!

Chapter 4 Solved!

First I landed on the cloud. Then I switched planes! I felt a queer feeling. I saw my plane following me with Amelia in it! Maybe my dream was REAL! All of a sudden a map popped on my lap and I followed it! I got out and Amelia did too! She told me to go home and she'd be watching me. She said never believe people who say they saw her. I felt special inside on my way home. When I picked my plane up I tied the planes together and Amelia's spirit became a part of me. And now I work with kids like Amelia did. When I started out I thought that Amelia was alive. She may be dead to others, but alive in me!

Judi Fay :: Grade 3
Frost Lake Elementary School :: St. Paul

Because

Because I ran the bases all spring,
   Dreams sprint wildly through my head.

Because I cut the water like a knife in summer,
   I slalom through the thickest problems.

Because in fall I donned a cast on my leg,
   A non-metallic armor guards my soul.

Because in winter the Basketball Court calls,
   I can dunk my fears out into space.

Aaron Weiche :: Grade 11
Buffalo Senior High School :: Buffalo

The Dream

Me and Carli got tired of thinking of ideas, so we decided to take a nap. I had a dream that a fairy godmother came to help me. She told me to get my ax out of the trunk of the car and cut the tree down. I thought that was a good idea. She was just about to leave when I quick asked her name and she said, "My name is Mariah Carey." I said, "You're my favorite female singer," and she said, "That's good, because I'm your fairy god mother." And then I said, "Well, then, I can see you whenever I want." "Yup, that's right. Just call 'fairy person come here.'"

Shawna Beise :: Grade 4
Lincoln Elementary School :: Brooklyn Park

The Goddess of Darkness

My sister is the goddess of darkness
she has fought the devil
she has made the time be as fast as a raging river and
    has power to tell the moon to rise and set.
she can make the sun take the life of the goodness of all
she takes the heart of the earth and makes it stop and
    twists blood out of it
she can take the sparkle away from the sun and take light
    away from Mars and the universe.

But in the real world, she is as powerless as an ant

Craig Sweet :: Grade 5
Eisenhower Elementary School :: Hopkins

Childhood

Childhood is like a car speeding on the highway
wild, crazy, running for your life, being chased
by a bully, then turning around and saying, "stop
you big bully," and then punching him and walking
away happier than ever.

Childhood is like a sunrise in the morning, cool, calm, relaxing
in a bunch of stuffed animals soft, warm, you lay
there until the evening sky and then doze,
doze, doze . . . z z z.

Jennifer Fenton :: Grade 4
Pullman Elementary School :: St. Paul Park

The Door Is Round and Open

Walking by the seashore
I see a glowing door
I can go through, or I don't.
The sun is shining brightly.
A man comes to me, he speaks:
"What you can see with your heart
you will never see with your eyes.
You can find a world that you imagine,
or you can keep your head out of the clouds.
You can go through the door,
but you will have to come out sometime."

I walk back into the real world
See the sea shore shining

The door is round and open.

Nikki Stevens :: Grade 5
Caledonia Elementary School :: Caledonia

Magic Present

May I come and show you my present
now, Mom? I rub my hands and apple trees
start growing in a day, and the apples are
already on, and they taste sweet.

Dustin Blonigen :: Grade 2
Avon Elementary School :: Avon

Where Laugh Touches Tears

To Keep Happiness

When you are happy,
You want to remember it.

You should take the happiness,
And objects, such as
A drawing from a child,
Or a stone from a walk along the beach,
And breathe the happiness into them,
Making sure every memory is there.

It will stay in these objects forever,
Locked up tight,
Until one day
You decide to unlock it,
And savor the happiness,
Breathing it back in.

Gretchen Mollers :: Grade 8
Central Middle School :: Columbia Heights

SAVER OF LIFE

I have laughed and squirmed with
restless chipmunks
I have scurried high in the storm's
clouds of death
I have seen what souls amount to
I have gazed past the stars to a world
of peace
I have seen hearts tear in two by
unkind souls

I have watched the spirits of fish
as they dive in and out
of the water of life
But instead of water
it was the mouth of God

Erika Olson :: Grade 5
Gatewood Elementary School :: Minnetonka

For You, My Friend

This is a poem for you, my friend.
You carry me over the wind
and through the trees.
You can run like the wind
and you can beat anything in a long race.
When you run through the swamp
you never sink in the mud.
You never yell at me
for all you can do is laugh.
You take me anywhere I want to go
with no complaints
and you take me there in a flash.
Oh, you may complain like a growl,
like a foolish cat, but you always stop
when it's time to go off
on our adventures
into the forest.

Katrina Cranston :: Grade 6
Pine Hill Elementary School :: Cottage Grove

It All Laughs

Flowers laugh in grass
Grass laughs in dirt
Dirt laughs in the earth
The earth laughs in space
Space laughs in the universe
And the universe laughs in nothing

Kelly McGuire :: Grade 2
Lakeview Elementary School :: Robbinsdale

Today's World

Emptiness, emptiness
I feel the emptiness in the world today,
like everyone has just died away
with the undying wind.
The world is so empty,
like a huge eating bowl,
like an empty daydream in the summer's day,
like doomsday has just fallen upon the earth,
like the fish taken, flooded with emptiness,
the fish no more.
I am gone with the world,
that is why I feel the cramming emptiness
in the world today.

Chad Carlson :: Grade 6
Pullman Elementary School :: St. Paul Park

Teddy Bear

A teddy bear sees so much,
Is told so much.

You think he will forget.
Those memories will always remain.

Children take advantage of teddy bears.
Adults take advantage of children.

I became the teddy bear.
No one knows what I know.

They did not see the childhood leaving
Like life leaves the teddy bear.

Monique Farness :: Grade 8
Richfield Junior High School :: Richfield

Being a Child

Childhood is like a piece of glass.
Sometimes it breaks to pieces.
When it gets glued together,
I can look through it and see Spring.

Matt Jensvold :: Grade 2
Centennial Elementary School :: Richfield

Asleep Forever

Tonight I am scared to death about
the death of my grandfather.
The way he looked at me
the last night I saw him.
His sunken icy blue eyes
pleading with me.
His wrinkled weak hand
reaching out to touch mine.
"Be a good kid."
He whispered through his dry lips.
The peaceful look on his
pale, made up face.
The suit I'd never seen on him
lying in the coffin.
He is now asleep forever,
his ashes deep in mother earth

Colleen Pemberton :: Grade 12
Buffalo High School :: Buffalo

A Lovely Dream

The dream I'd like to have would be one for my dad. I'd like to dream that he'd be well, not lying on his back. Where he could walk, and we could talk of days left in the past. We could take the family out and all roll in the grass. We could stop and smell the roses and listen to the birdies sing, we could throw a ball or two, and laugh at funny things. We could all be together just like a family. But when I awoke it was no joke but the end of a lovely dream.

Georgina Sisk :: Grade 6
Sandstone Elementary School :: Sandstone

Masks

I wear this mask of happy
not for my sake, but for you
You see me as a joker
from my masked point of view
My life must always be happy
My attitude a laugh
This is a part of me
but you're only seeing half
My life's a one-liner
a joke, a smile, never a tear or frown
I am a person with your reputation
of never being down
Even when I have bad days
I can't show them to you
Just once, I'd like you to see me
From an unmasked point of view

Cory Busse :: Grade 12
Prior Lake High School :: Prior Lake

Maybe This Way Is Better

The slamming of the car door signals the end of another "vacation" with Dad. He watches the red tail lights dim in the distance through the blur of tears. Life is unfair. Why does everything sooner or later have to end?

He walks slowly to the house kicking rocks that have strayed onto the sidewalk. Stalling. As if by keeping distance between himself and reality, it will not proceed. But it is no use. The reality is Brandon won't see his father for two whole weeks. That's half a month. No one seems to understand the awesome weight that puts upon himself.

Closing the door carefully does not stop his mother from hearing him enter.

"Honey, is that you?"

"Ya, Mom," he calls back loud enough for her to hear over the TV. That's where she always seems to be lately—in the family room lounging on the flowered couch staring blankly at the TV screen. Family room. What a joke! What kind of a family is split up into two separate units? And the hard part is, he's expected to be involved in both divisions. Brandon can't handle that. He feels as if unknowingly both parents are pulling at his emotions. Forcing himself to choose between them.

Brandon makes his way up the plush carpeted stairs toward his bedroom. His tired eyes wander over to a framed photograph hanging on the wall. Mom, Dad, Brandon. All smiling widely. An outsider would look at the picture and probably comment: "My what a nice looking family. It's refreshing to see a family which is actually happy and that truly loves each other." Now the photo only causes a wince of pain through Brandon's heart. A thought comes into his mind. "I wonder if even then those smiles were fake? How long was I blind to what was really going on? Darn them! Why didn't they love each other enough to try? Why didn't they love *me* enough to give it a second chance?"

Upstairs in his bedroom, Brandon unpacks his suitcase. Staring up at him are all the mementos from the past weekend.

Stubs from the double feature movie they went to see. The new Twins T-shirt already blemished by the chocolate ice cream cone they ate while walking through the park talking. The church bulletin from this morning containing the songs they didn't know — yet for some reason they sang anyway. And one more thing. Brandon reaches deep into his jean pocket and pulls out a small gold cross. He relives the moment when Dad gave it to him.

They had just gotten back in the car after their lunch at Pizza Hut. Brandon was talking excitedly about the afternoon that lay ahead.

"Hey, Hey! Slow down. We'll get to that in a minute. I want to talk to you seriously for a while. Okay?"

"Okay, Dad." Brandon felt the urge to jump out of the car and take off. He knew what was coming and he didn't want to be around to hear it.

"Well . . . ah . . . you see, Brandon. . . . Look I guess what I want you to know is I'm sorry. This divorce has been unfair to you but I think we made the best choice in separating. It would be worse for you to live in a place where all you heard was fighting. I mean—"

Suddenly Brandon heard himself explode at his father. "How do you know? How do you know what would've been better for me? Did anyone ask me? No! You were just being selfish thinking of yourself. I could have handled the yelling. What I can't deal with is not being able to see you when I want to. Yah, I'm just real sure I'm happier now!" Brandon's voice was filled with bitterness and sarcasm. He had shocked himself at first but now he was mad. He wasn't crying but he almost wished he was since it would have covered up the loud harsh silence that engulfed them.

Finally, Brandon's dad took his hand and placed the cross on his palm. He mentioned something about wanting him to have this, phrases of "when I'm not around" and "maybe this will help." But Brandon didn't hardly hear a word his father said. All he felt was a tremendous sense of aloneness as he smelled the tangy spices from the pizza they had brought with them. For some reason the aroma was very strong now. He held his head in his hands as he thought to himself, "I am going to be sick."

They had finally made up and by the time his dad dropped him off Brandon was ready to give him a hug good-bye. As he looks at the cross now in his room, he smiles sadly to himself. No amount of gifts—even a cross—would make up for his father's absence.

A knock on the door forces himself to stop his depression for a while.

"Hi. I was just wondering how it went with your dad."

"Fine. He said to say hi and hopes you're doing well."

"What does he mean by saying that? He's being sarcastic just hoping to annoy me? Why can't he just leave me alone!" Brandon's mother's voice was first accusing and then was loudening into a rage.

"Hey, Mom. Cool it, all right? Dad meant exactly what he said. He wasn't trying to do anything except get along with you. That's it."

"Okay, I'm sorry. I guess I just haven't had a good weekend. I'm sorry I got upset. I missed you this weekend you know."

Brandon's mother grabs him and gives him a hug. Brandon pats his mother on the back and says, "Ya, Mom. I know."

"Let's go downstairs now. Supper is ready."

"Ya. I'll be there in a minute."

As she closes the door behind her, Brandon thinks to himself, "Maybe Dad was right. Maybe this way is better for everyone. To have my parents separated and actually still be happy. Well I suppose it's worth a shot."

As Brandon walked down the stairs, he smells a familiar blend of tangy spices. "Pizza. We're having pizza for supper." Brandon laughs to himself quietly. On the bottom step he stops to pull out his cross from his pocket and look at it one more time. This time he doesn't feel alone or sick. Instead, he smiles his first genuine smile in a long time.

Diane Strandlund :: Grade 12
Roseau High School :: Roseau

More Than Just a Regular Day

It seemed like just a regular day. The birds were singing, wind blowing and Mom making a fresh apple pie. I walked up the stairs and saw my mom, the big belly bulging out of the apron. The belly that held my new brother or sister. I walked up to my mom and gave her a hug and said good morning. It *was* a regular day. At about noon, Mommy said she was going to lie down for a bit and Grandma would come over and play with me. Grandma came and made me lunch and we played. But it wasn't very much fun, because every now and then I would hear Mommy crying, or moaning as if in pain. I wanted to help her but Grandma wouldn't let me in. Me and Grandma were watching TV and having a snack when Daddy came home. It was only 3:00 p.m. He's not supposed to come home 'til 5:00 I thought. But I was just happy to see him. He looked like he was happy to see me, but when I went to hug him, he had gone to see Mommy already. I started to run into the bedroom but Grandma said no. Daddy came out and so did Mommy. They said they had to leave for a while and that when they came home they would bring me something, and that I should be a good girl for Grandma and then maybe I could go see them. That got me excited. I begged my Grandma to tell me what was going on because I was getting really confused. She told me what was going on because it was time for Mom to have my little brother or sister. Oh, wow! I thought. My new brother or sister. I ran to the baby's room and started dancing. I didn't realize it at first but I thought I heard Grandma crying. I ran to see what was wrong. I asked her. She said, "My dear child, your mother is having a child, my *2nd* grandchild, do you know what that means?" I shook my head.

"It means I'm getting old. I am not young any more. I miss being young and dancing around like you, Heather."

I couldn't say anything that I thought would make Grandma feel better, so I just laid my head down on her lap and said, "I'm sorry you don't want me Grandma."

She cried harder now and said, "Oh, no, sweetheart, I love you more than anything and don't you ever think different."

I think she might have kept talking but I fell asleep. And she must have felt better because when I woke up, supper was on the table and she said, "After supper, let's go and see your new brother, Jon."

A brother! Oh, I was so excited I could barely eat, but man, was I hungry. So I ate fast. Then Grandma did my hair nice, and we went to the hospital. When I first saw Mommy she looked tired, so I ran over and said, "Are you okay, Mommy?" She said she was terrific. Then the nurse came in and handed the bundle of joy in my Mom's arms. I peeked in the little blanket and saw what has changed my life. The little face with its tiny nose and closed eyes. The little fingers that held tightly onto mine. This was my brother, and he was beautiful. Now when we got him home he would cry and have to be fed or held and didn't seem quite as beautiful but we still all loved Jon.

Heather Milless :: Grade 10
Elk River Senior High School :: Elk River

Ranae

Ranae. . . .

An album of tearful, loving memories
A flower blowing in the wind.

Ranae. . . .

Like a book with no pages, a rose with
no petals, a clock with no time.

Ranae. . . .

A diary of thought, excitement, sadness,
My life drifts by like a dream
When I wake up, I realize that
My life is gone, gone like a summer rain.

Ranae. . . .

Like a calm meadow with a whistling
wind swirling around the air.
A growing tree, waiting to grow up.

Ranae. . . .

Tell me, who am I, what am I doing here?
Now all I am is an old light, flickering
flickering into darkness.

Ranae Wayrynen :: Grade 5
McGregor Schools :: McGregor

After Surgery

I walked into the recovery room
in intensive care.
It was cold and white
There was a pitch black silence
The only noise was the time bomb
carbon valve
The only color was the yellow flower
that was like a candle
at the center of the darkest cave
I looked at my dad
He was like a flag with bullet holes through it
on a windless day
He was like a quiet rabbit
And the valve kept ticking.

Jake Mulligan :: Grade 6
Pilot Knob Elementary School :: Eagan

Losing a Pet

I want to speak about losing a pet.
On a day when you lose a pet
the sky turns gray like a dead forest
that is still smoking.
You don't feel the silky touch of a blade of grass
or smell the flowers.
But you feel like you are in a deep dark cave
with rocks to walk on
and musty air to smell.
Instead of hearing joyful sounds
the sounds you hear are low, dark and spooky.
All of a sudden your joyful self
is alone and feeling afraid
in a black, wet, endless cave of loneliness
with no one to look to or turn to.

Jessica Koll :: Grade 4
Belle Plaine Elementary School :: Belle Plaine

Matching Pair of Eyes

There was a little blind girl. She wanted so much to find her lost eyesight. So one day she put on her stitched brown leathery shoes and started her search. The big blue sky looked wonderful, but she did not know that. She was looking and feeling almost everything when she came across a ridged rock. It was shattered with edges as sharp as the blazing sky, but that wasn't it. She listened to the beautiful birds singing their magical songs. And all of a sudden she heard a little voice. It sounded so much like a piano singing in high key of C. Oh, she ran like mad 'til she was at her home again. She could still hear the voice crying out to her. As she opened the door, she heard the hinges squeak. She stumbled over something. She knelt down and felt something. It was a locket and then she knew that she would probably never see again, but she had found her matching pair of eyes.

Jamie Ager :: Grade 6
Long Prairie Elementary School :: Long Prairie

Red Licorice

Ah, red licorice, a string of which is
the perfect length for wrapping around
a pale slender neck in a nice tight knot.

The sun beats down on the melting red licorice
waiting for an unsuspecting shoe to tread
upon it.

But to look at life through the hole of a strand of red licorice.

The mountains may crumble,
the oceans may dry to a barren field of sand,
but the red licorice will live on forever.

Reeking rhino with rippling rolls
of retained root beer
running reverently
racing to reach the red licorice

The iguanas that were in
the bathrooms of Botswana
are being shipped to Antarctic
to share it with the polar bears

Looking into the eyes of my love
I see
red licorice.

Nibbling on opposite ends
of a strand of red licorice
his bites became suspiciously larger.

Nothing cuts the heat
of a Saudi Arabian desert
like a strand of red licorice.

To a child
what could be savored more
than a piece of red licorice
after a hard-earned quarter
has been placed on the counter.

Tricia Roberts :: Grade 10
Richfield High School :: Richfield

Where Laughter Touches Tears

I have gone to where my laughter talks
to my tears,
Where dawn meets twilight,
And where the sky touches the last
layer of the earth.
Where Hawk and Eagle don't fight
Over their prey,
I have seen a drought turn into a
Flood.
I have gone to where my laughter
talks to my tears.

Kelli Beitlich :: Grade 5
Alice Smith Elementary School :: Hopkins

Author Index

Kara Adams	Blake Middle School	14
Jamie Ager	Long Prairie Elementary School	152
Mychal Lynn Anderson	Glen Lake Elementary School	105
Tammy Anderson	Mankato East High School	25
Eric Andrews	Oltman Junior High School	102
Azra Babar	Willow River School	51
Sean Bauch	Fred Moore Junior High School	47
Shawna Beise	Lincoln Elementary School	127
Kelli Beitlich	Alice Smith Elementary School	155
Ryan Bigelow	Lakeview Elementary School	38
Hannah Blair	Lake Country School	42
Dustin Blonigen	Avon Elementary School	131
Christy Boraas	Madison Elementary School	67
Matthew P. Borg	Lincoln Elementary School	80
Rachel Breitenbach	Winston Churchill Elementary School	81
Dee Dee Budde	Central Middle School	77
Andrew Burth	Newport Elementary School	89
Cory Busse	Prior Lake High School	143
Chad Carlson	Pullman Elementary School	138
Jessica Carlson	Royal Oaks Elementary School	8
Adam Cerling	Farmington Middle School	50
Sotearit Chak	Cherokee Heights Elementary School	93
Zack Chapman	Tanglen Elementary School	10
Dan Compton	Deerwood Elementary School	90
Katrina Cranston	Pine Hill Elementary School	136
Eva Curry	Annunciation School	23
Brian Daniels	Royal Oaks Elementary School	46
Lori DeLaitsch	Central Middle School	76
Jared Detloff	Swanville Public School	57
Kara Marie Dinkel	Long Prairie Elementary School	6
Tamara Eagle	Heart of the Earth Survival School	109
Clayton Engen	Aquila Primary Center	99

Monique Farness	Richfield Junior High School 139
Judi Fay	Frost Lake Elementary School 124
Jennifer Fenton	Pullman Elementary School 129
Teri Firkins	Fairmont High School 59
Dina Fuerstenberg	Stillwater High School 7
Molly Gilberg	Barnum Elementary School 2
Michelle Gilbert	Guadalupe Area Project 92
Karen Gilbertson	Mankato East Junior High School 119
Liz Goodman	Blake Middle School 64
Jennie Grundeen	Shirley Hills Elementary School 114
Mark Gudmastad	Central Elementary School 113
Makalah Haessler	Castle Elementary School 88
Scott Hella	Lanesboro Public School 40
Jason Helm	John Adams Junior High School 3
Liz Hook	Our Lady of the Lake School 33
Tony Housey	Woodland Junior High School 104
Travis Howard	Rockford High School 29
Carolyn Hudella	Oltman Junior High School 103
Fong Inthavixay	Worthington Junior High School 58
Nkoyo E. Iyamba	Convent of the Visitation School 36
Gina Jaszczak	Oltman Junior High School 115
Matt Jensvold	Centennial Elementary School 140
Barry Jesinoski	Battle Lake School 24
Christina Joeckel	Pullman Elementary School 12
Orin Johnson	RTR High School 70
Nancy Kadlec	McGregor School 97
John Kent	North Elementary School 45
Rich Kirk	Oltman Junior High School 37
Deanne Kociemba	Holdingford Elementary School 120
Nicole Kolashinski	Woodbury Middle School 118
Jessica Koll	Belle Plaine Elementary School 151
Marni Kramer	GFW High School 53
Virginia Laursen	Madison Elementary School 48
Malla Lofgren	Shirley Hills Elementary School 9
Missy Lund	Woodbury Middle School 27
Kelly McGuire	Lakeview Elementary School 137
Jessica McKinley	Benjamin E. Mays School 63
Shayne B. Meyer	Sandstone Elementary School 98

Magenta Miller	Northrop Montessori School 85
Heather Milless	Elk River High School 147
John Mitsch	St. Rose of Lima School 39
Gretchen Mollers	Central Middle School 134
Missy Mollick	Kennedy Elementary School 79
Aaron Morrison	Katherine Curren Elementary School 110
Jake Mulligan	Pilot Knob Elementary School 150
Tracey Muralt	Elm Creek Elementary School 78
Erika Olson	Gatewood Elementary School 135
Kelsey Olson	Appleton Elementary School 69
Colleen Pemberton	Buffalo High School 141
Aaron Peter	Elmore Elementary School 68
Tonya Peterson	Long Prairie High School 19
Joshua Pierce	Woodbury Elementary School 13
John Poegel	Swanville Public School 86
Nina Raulerson	Cherokee Heights Elementary School 96
Stacy Reed	Cherokee Heights Elementary School 94
Brigit Riley	Central Middle School 49
Tricia Roberts	Richfield High School 153
Derek Schluessler	Christa McAuliffe Elementary School 5
Dan Schwarz	LeSueur Junior High School 91
Mara Segal	Meadowbrook Elementary School 41
Nkenge Ayoka Shakir	Benjamin E. Mays School 61
Kevin Sieben	Pinecrest Elementary School 121
Georgina Sisk	Sandstone Elementary School 142
Cindy Skogerboe	Sand Creek Elementary School 74
Naomi Smith	Benjamin E. Mays School 107
Michael Spencer	Benjamin E. Mays School 62
Kari Spielman	Balaton School 28
Rachel Squires	Woodbury Middle School 84
Nikki Stevens	Caledonia Elementary School 130
Jeremy Stewart	Hillside Elementary School 112
Diane Strandlund	Roseau High School 144

Ricky Sullivan	St. Rose of Lima School	39
Craig Sweet	Eisenhower Elementary School	128
Jim Vanderbeek	Oltman Junior High School	22
Minne Vang	Cherokee Heights Elementary School	95
Ranae Wayrynen	McGregor School	149
Aaron Weckman	Jordon Elementary School	44
Aaron Weiche	Buffalo High School	126
Jennifer Wetherbee	Oak Grove Intermediate School	82
Natalie White	Elton Hills Elementary School	87
Chaitra Wirta	Weaver School	122

School Index

Alice Smith Elementary School
Appleton Elementary School
Annunciation School
Aquila Primary Center
Avon Elementary School
Balaton School
Barnum Elementary School
Battle Lake School
Belle Plaine Elementary School
Benjamin E. Mays School
Benjamin E. Mays School
Benjamin E. Mays School
Benjamin E. Mays School
Blake Middle School
Blake Middle School
Buffalo High School
Buffalo High School
Caledonia Elementary School
Castle Elementary School
Centennial Elementary School
Central Elementary School
Central Middle School
Central Middle School
Central Middle School
Central Middle School
Cherokee Heights Elementary School
Cherokee Heights Elementary School
Cherokee Heights Elementary School
Cherokee Heights Elementary School
Christa McAuliffe Elementary School

Kelli Beitlich 155
Kelsey Olson..................69
Eva Curry 23
Clayton Engen 99
Dustin Blonigen 131
Kari Spielman................28
Molly Gilberg 2
Barry Jesinoski 24
Jessica Koll 151
Jessica McKinley 63
Nkenge Ayoka Shakir 61
Naomi Smith................107
Michael Spencer 62
Kara Adams...................14
Liz Goodman 64
Colleen Pemberton.......141
Aaron Weiche...............126
Nikki Stevens...............130
Makalah Haessler 88
Matt Jensvold 140
Mark Gudmastad 113
Dee Dee Budde.............77
Lori DeLaitsch 76
Gretchen Mollers 134
Brigit Riley 49

Sotearit Chak 93

Nina Raulerson 96

Stacy Reed.....................94

Minne Vang 95

Derek Schluessler.............5

Where Laugh Touches Tears :: 161

Convent of the Visitation School
Deerwood Elementary School
Eisenhower Elementary School
Elk River High School
Elm Creek Elementary School
Elmore Elementary School
Elton Hills Elementary School
Fairmont High School
Farmington Middle School
Fred Moore Junior High School
Frost Lake Elementary School
Gatewood Elementary School
GFW High School
Glen Lake Elementary School
Guadalupe Area Project
Heart of the Earth Survival School
Hillside Elementary School
Holdingford Elementary School
John Adams Junior High School
Jordon Elementary School
Katherine Curren Elementary School
Kennedy Elementary School
Lake Country School
Lakeview Elementary School
Lakeview Elementary School
Lanesboro Public School
LeSueur Junior High School
Lincoln Elementary School
Lincoln Elementary School
Long Prairie Elementary School
Long Prairie Elementary School
Long Prairie High School
Madison Elementary School
Madison Elementary School
Mankato East High School
Mankato East Junior High School
McGregor School

Nkoyo E. Iyamba............36
Dan Compton................90
Craig Sweet..................128
Heather Milless 147
Tracey Muralt 78
Aaron Peter....................68
Natalie White 87
Teri Firkins 59
Adam Cerling 50
Sean Bauch....................47
Judi Fay........................124
Erika Olson..................135
Marni Kramer 53
Mychal Lynn Anderson 105
Michelle Gilbert 92
Tamara Eagle................109
Jeremy Stewart.............112
Deanne Kociemba 120
Jason Helm......................3
Aaron Weckman 44

Aaron Morrison 110
Missy Mollick 79
Hannah Blair..................42
Ryan Bigelow 38
Kelly McGuire 137
Scott Hella 40
Dan Schwarz..................91
Shawna Beise 127
Matthew P. Borg 80
Jamie Ager....................152
Kara Marie Dinkel 6
Tonya Peterson 19
Christy Boraas 67
Virginia Laursen.............48
Tammy Anderson 25
Karen Gilbertson..........119
Nancy Kadlec.................97

McGregor School	Ranae Wayrynen 149
Meadowbrook Elementary School	Mara Segal 41
Newport Elementary School	Andrew Burth................89
North Elementary School	John Kent......................45
Northrop Montessori School	Magenta Miller 85
Oak Grove Intermediate School	Jennifer Wetherbee.........82
Oltman Junior High School	Eric Andrews 102
Oltman Junior High School	Carolyn Hudella...........103
Oltman Junior High School	Gina Jaszczak................115
Oltman Junior High School	Rich Kirk 37
Oltman Junior High School	Jim Vanderbeek...............22
Our Lady of the Lake School	Liz Hook.......................33
Pilot Knob Elementary School	Jake Mulligan 150
Pine Hill Elementary School	Katrina Cranston..........139
Pinecrest Elementary School	Kevin Sieben 121
Prior Lake High School	Cory Busse...................143
Pullman Elementary School	Chad Carlson 138
Pullman Elementary School	Jennifer Fenton............129
Pullman Elementary School	Christina Joeckel 12
Richfield High School	Tricia Roberts...............153
Richfield Junior High School	Monique Farness..........136
Rockford High School	Travis Howard................29
Roseau High School	Diane Strandlund 144
Royal Oaks Elementary School	Jessica Carlson.................8
Royal Oaks Elementary School	Brian Daniels.................46
RTR High School	Orin Johnson 70
St. Rose of Lima School	John Mitsch....................39
St. Rose of Lima School	Ricky Sullivan................39
Sand Creek Elementary School	Cindy Skogerboe 74
Sandstone Elementary School	Shayne B. Meyer............98
Sandstone Elementary School	Georgina Sisk...............142
Shirley Hills Elementary School	Jennie Grundeen...........114
Shirley Hills Elementary School	Malla Lofgren 9
Stillwater High School	Dina Fuerstenberg............7
Swanville Public School	Jared Detloff...................57
Swanville Public School	John Poegel....................86
Tanglen Elementary School	Zack Chapman................10
Weaver School	Chaitra Wirta 122

WHERE LAUGH TOUCHES TEARS :: 163

Willow River School	Azra Babar 51
Winston Churchill Elementary School	Rachel Breitenbach.........81
Woodbury Elementary School	Joshua Pierce 13
Woodbury Middle School	Nicole Kolashinski 118
Woodbury Middle School	Missy Lund 27
Woodbury Middle School	Rachel Squires 84
Woodland Junior High School	Tony Housey 104
Worthington Junior High School	Fong Inthavixay.............58

Program Writers 1990–91

Sigrid Bergie
John Caddy
Florence Chard Dacey
Kate Dayton
Daniel Gabriel
Margot Fortunato Galt
Ellen Hawley
Dana Jensen
Gita Kar
Jane Katz
Judith Katz
Roseann Lloyd
Roy McBride
Ken Meter
Jaime Meyer
John Minczeski
Jim Northrup, Jr.
Sheila O'Connor
Joe Paddock
Nancy Paddock
Alexs Pate
Stephen Peters
Mary Rockcastle
Ruth Roston
Mary Kay Rummel
Richard Solly
Deborah Stein
Susan Marie Swanson
Linda Wing